Nothing is Impossible

The Legend of Joe Hardy and 84 Lumber

Nothing is Impossible

The Legend of Joe Hardy and 84 Lumber

Jeffrey L. Rodengen

Edited by Amy Bush & Jill Gambill
Design and layout by Dennis Shockley & Rachelle Donley

Write Stuff Enterprises, Inc.
1001 South Andrews Avenue
Fort Lauderdale, FL 33316
1-800-900-Book (1-800-900-2665)
(954) 462-6657
www.writestuffbooks.com

Publisher's Cataloging in Publication Data
(Prepared by The Donohue Group, Inc.)

Rodengen, Jeffrey L.
     Nothing is impossible : the legend of Joe Hardy and 84 Lumber / Jeffrey L. Rodengen ; edited by Amy Bush & Jill Gambill ; design and layout by Dennis Shockley & Rachelle Donley.

     p. : ill. ; cm.
     Includes bibliographical references and index.
     ISBN: 1-932022-07-4

1. Hardy, Joseph A., III. 2. 84 Lumber (Firm)
3. Businesspeople—Pennsylvania—Biography.
4. Chief executive officers—Pennsylvania—
Biography. 5. Lumber trade—Pennsylvania—
History. 6. Hardware industry—Pennsylvania—
History. 7. Building materials industry—
Pennsylvania—History. I. Bush, Amy. II. Jill
Gambill III. Shockley, Dennis. IV. Donley,
Rachelle. V. Title.

HD9760.H37 R63 2005
338.476/74/092   2005929939

Completely produced in the
United States of America
10 9 8 7 6 5 4 3 2 1

Also by Jeffrey L. Rodengen

The Legend of Chris-Craft

IRON FIST:
The Lives of Carl Kiekhaefer

Evinrude-Johnson
and The Legend of OMC

Serving the Silent Service:
The Legend of Electric Boat

The Legend of Dr Pepper/Seven-Up

The Legend of Honeywell

The Legend of Briggs & Stratton

The Legend of Ingersoll-Rand

The Legend of Stanley:
150 Years of The Stanley Works

The MicroAge Way

The Legend of Halliburton

The Legend of York International

The Legend of Nucor Corporation

The Legend of Goodyear:
The First 100 Years

The Legend of AMP

The Legend of Cessna

The Legend of VF Corporation

The Spirit of AMD

The Legend of Rowan

New Horizons:
The Story of Ashland Inc.

The History of American Standard

The Legend of Mercury Marine

The Legend of Federal-Mogul

Against the Odds:
Inter-Tel—The First 30 Years

The Legend of Pfizer

State of the Heart:
The Practical Guide to Your Heart
and Heart Surgery
with Larry W. Stephenson, M.D.

The Legend of
Worthington Industries

The Legend of IBP, Inc.

The Legend of
Trinity Industries, Inc.

The Legend of
Cornelius Vanderbilt Whitney

The Legend of Amdahl

The Legend of Litton Industries

The Legend of Gulfstream

The Legend of Bertram
with David A. Patten

The Legend of
Ritchie Bros. Auctioneers

The Legend of ALLTEL
with David A. Patten

The Yes, you can of
Invacare Corporation
with Anthony L. Wall

The Ship in the Balloon:
The Story of Boston Scientific
and the Development of
Less-Invasive Medicine

The Legend of Day & Zimmermann

The Legend of Noble Drilling

Fifty Years of Innovation:
Kulicke & Soffa

Biomet—From Warsaw
to the World
with Richard F. Hubbard

NRA: An American Legend

The Heritage and Values
of RPM, Inc.

The Marmon Group:
The First Fifty Years

The Legend of Grainger

The Legend of
The Titan Corporation
with Richard F. Hubbard

The Legend of Discount Tire Co.
with Richard F. Hubbard

The Legend of Polaris
with Richard F. Hubbard

The Legend of La-Z-Boy
with Richard F. Hubbard

The Legend of McCarthy
with Richard F. Hubbard

InterVoice:
Twenty Years of Innovation
with Richard F. Hubbard

Jefferson-Pilot Financial:
A Century of Excellence
with Richard F. Hubbard

The Legend of HCA
with Richard F. Hubbard

The Legend of Werner Enterprises
with Richard F. Hubbard

The History of J. F. Shea Co.
with Richard F. Hubbard

True to Our Vision
with Richard F. Hubbard

Albert Trostel & Sons
with Richard F. Hubbard

The Legend of Guardian Industries

The Legend of
Universal Forest Products

Polytechnic University: Changing
the World—The First 150 Years

In It For The Long Haul:
The Story of CRST

TABLE OF CONTENTS

FOREWORD

BY
TOM RIDGE
FIRST SECRETARY OF HOMELAND SECURITY

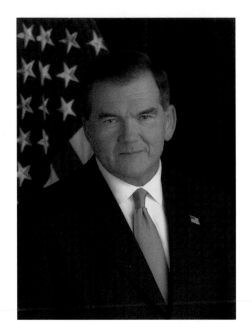

WHEN I FIRST RAN FOR governor of Pennsylvania more than 10 years ago, among the first people I went to see was Joe Hardy. At first blush, Eighty Four, Pennsylvania, headquarters for 84 Lumber, may not seem like an important destination. It's certainly not the most populous region in the state, but many people who run for office here soon realize that meeting Joe—and earning his trust and support—is critical. Joe is a man who gets things done. Really, nothing—*nothing*—is impossible for this remarkable entrepreneur.

Joe, at the young age of fourscore years, decided to run for county commissioner of Fayette County. The voter registration was 3- or 4-to-1 against his party. Even against the odds, I figured he would win. Let me tell you why. When young people seek advice about politics, I emphasize patience and participation. I encourage them to return to their communities and contribute in a personal and professional way. I also stress the need to work hard to earn the people's trust. The community needs to understand that you care, before they care what you know. Joe won because he had been working hard to earn the community's trust almost from the first day he went into business. Everyone understands that Joe truly cares.

Joe is also a wonderful collection of contradictions. There is an 84 Lumber location less than a mile from my house. It's an all-business, no-nonsense operation. In December and January, the sales staff and customers alike are wearing coats and gloves because there is no heat in the place. But everything you need is there, and you're not paying a premium for all the extras. No more, no less. Joe is much like that, too. What you see is what you get. You don't have to wonder if there is some ulterior motive, some hidden agenda, or some unexpressed purpose.

But then there is another side of Joe that's the polar opposite of his unadorned personality. Joe's magnificent Nemacolin Woodlands Resort is among the most beautiful, opulent, artistic, and exquisitely detailed resort destinations in the world. When Joe purchased what was a modest facility in 1987, he said, "Someday this will be among the finest resorts in the world," and many people wondered, "Can he be serious?"

Nearly 20 years and over $100 million later, no one doubts his sincerity or his ability to accomplish whatever his sets his mind to doing. Nemacolin Woodlands Resort today boasts two of the most beautiful golf courses in the state, one a regular stop on the PGA Tour for the 84 Lumber Classic; the magnificent Chateau LaFayette, a replica of the Ritz Hotel in Paris; as well as the Mystic Mountain ski resort, shopping arcade, skeet range, equestrian center, gourmet restaurants, and more. The resort also boasts one of the most luxurious spas in the nation, adorned with what seems like a sea of marble. Every year, Joe hosts a Royal Reception at the resort, attended by dukes, duchesses, barons and baronesses.

As Joe took his oath of office as Fayette County commissioner, it wasn't long before a discussion began about what could be done to help the city of Uniontown, Pennsylvania. Like many small American cities, its downtown business district, once a bustling commercial zone, had slowly atrophied as competing businesses opened in expansive malls in the suburbs. Joe brought his idea for a massive rejuvenation project to the table, and his fellow commissioners agreed that it would be great, but there were limited funds available. "That's O.K.," Joe responded. "I'll just fund it myself." Joe immediately began to research how other communities had accomplished similar goals. "How long did it take?" Joe would ask. When the answer came back, "Ten to 12 years," Joe said, "I'll do it in as many months." Impossible? You're starting to get the picture.

Joe assumed command of the project, code-named the Marshall Plan II, after the enormous reconstruction of Germany following World War II. He formed a company to manage the streetscaping effort and pledged $1 million of his own to kick-start the campaign. Soon, storefronts were being repaired and painted, damaged sidewalks were replaced, new lampposts sprouted, and Joe was just picking up steam. He provided additional matching funds for businesses eager to improve their properties, and the city of Uniontown provided no-interest loans to help with the balance. In all, Joe quietly contributed over $4 million to the renovation. And the best part? Joe completed the dramatic face-lifting first phase in an astounding 90 days. Seems impossible, doesn't it?

From the very beginning, Joe built the business of 84 Lumber on a philosophy of fairness and service. Whatever the customer needed, Joe would supply. If contractors needed staggered deliveries of building materials, Joe would accommodate them. If a single two-by-four was defective in a truckload of lumber, Joe would replace it. If a contractor said he could save a few cents a foot with another supplier, Joe would research it, and if true, match it. Stories abound of Joe's determination to make 84 Lumber the best in the business. It was a solid philosophy and a thriving business, but one day, Joe decided to completely change the business. Impossible?

When terrorists struck the heart of America on September 11, 2001, killing and wounding thousands from New York to Washington, D.C., to Pennsylvania, it was a frightening wake-up call for all Americans. We found out we were vulnerable. We had not anticipated the ruthless abandon of the terrorists. Much had to change, and quickly. From increased airport security to closer communication between our intelligence services, America answered the call to action.

But oftentimes in business, there is no defining moment, no catastrophic event to galvanize a leader. And so it was for Joe as 84 Lumber continued to grow into a nationwide chain of do-it-yourself outlets, catering primarily to the needs of the weekend home remodeler, selling everything from nails to the kitchen sink. But the industry was changing. New megastores were adding locations throughout the country, investing hundreds of millions of dollars to offer the same formula of inexpensive products and services that Joe had helped to pioneer for years. So one day in 1991, Joe announced to his senior staff that 84 Lumber would return to its roots, concentrating its efforts on the professional contractor and homebuilder—the very first customers served by 84 lumber. Impossible? Not for Joe.

In a rolling restructuring process worthy of a major military campaign, Joe managed to completely transform 84 Lumber. Within months, the company had begun to re-establish relationships with professional contractors, and rebuild the supply chains necessary to service the newly defined market.

Joe is the model for the advice I give young citizens wanting to serve through politics. This book is a fitting tribute to one who has done so much to improve the lives of millions, from customers and employees, to constituents and neighbors. The only thing impossible about Joe is that it is impossible that he will ever be forgotten.

ACKNOWLEDGMENTS

MANY DEDICATED PROFESSIONALS assisted in the research, preparation, and publication of *Nothing Is Impossible: The Legend of Joe Hardy and 84 Lumber.*

The principal research and assembly of the narrative timeline was accomplished by research assistant Anjali Sachdeva. Senior Editors Amy Bush and Jill Gambill oversaw the text and photos, and the graphic design of Art Director Dennis Shockley brought the story to life.

A number of key people associated with 84 Lumber lent their efforts to the book's completion, sharing their experiences, providing valuable oversight for accuracy, and helping guide the book's development from outline to final form: Joe Hardy, founder; Maggie Hardy Magerko, president; Bill Myrick, chief operating officer; Frank Cicero, vice president of store operations; Dan Wallach, chief financial officer; Cheri Bomar, attorney/development director; and Michelle Lee, assistant to the president.

Many other executives, employees, colleagues, retirees, and family members enriched the book by discussing their experiences. The author extends particular gratitude to these men and women for their candid recollections and guidance: Wanda Anker, Ray Barley, Gail Baughman, Denny Brua, Nan Cameron, Terry Carter, Greg Clark, William Conover, Donna Criss, Bud Dolfi, Helen Dolfi, Judy Donahue, Phil Drake, Joe Ferens, Mike Figgins, Robin Freed, Bill Fulton, Jim Punyak, Don Gearhart, Betty Gottschallt, Cecil Gravely, Jim Guest, Virginia Hackman, Alex Hardy, Bob Hardy, Debbie Hardy, Dan Hixenbaugh, Craig Johnson, Bob Junk, Jerry King, Jack Klema, Jeff Kmiec, Jack Knight, Bill Lincoln, Nick Ludi, Bob MacKinney, Bernie Magerko, Pete Magerko, Jerry Maley Sr., Bob Martik, Dean Martik, Trey Matheu, Sid McAllister, Jim McCorkle, Charles Moore, Barbara Mosi, Chris Pournaras, Rose Pournaras, Ed Ryan, Norma Ryan, Charmaine Sampson, Barbara Stork, Jeanene Tomshay, Christina Toras, Bill Underdonk, Vince Vicites, Bud Weber, Chip Young, Nancy Young, Jim Zaunick, and Harry Zeune.

Special thanks is extended to the staff and associates at Write Stuff Enterprises, Inc.: Stanimira "Sam" Stefanova, executive editor; Mickey Murphy and Ann Gossy, senior editors; Kevin Allen and Martin Schultz, proofreaders; Sandy Cruz, vice president/creative director; Rachelle Donley, art director; Mary Aaron, transcriptionist; Barbara Koch, indexer; Marianne Roberts, executive vice president of publishing and chief financial officer; Amy Major, executive assistant to Jeffrey L. Rodengen; Steven Stahl, director of marketing; and Sherry Hasso, bookkeeper. Richard F. Hubbard conducted additional interviews.

When Pittsburgh's steel industry was booming, clouds of smog hung over the city at all hours. This "night" scene from the 1940s was taken before noon. Residents saw the pollution as a sign that the local mills were productive and the economic outlook for the area was favorable. *(Photo courtesy of Library and Archives Division, Historical Society of Western Pennsylvania, Pittsburgh, PA)*

CHAPTER ONE

FOUNDATIONS FOR SUCCESS

I don't think she graduated from high school, my mother, but if I would mess around with some jerks, whatever you'd call them today, she'd say, "What are you fooling around with those people for?" And I said, "Gee, Mom, they're a lot of fun. They're fun, fun, fun." She said, "Knock it off. You're something special, and you're going to amount to something."

—Joe Hardy, founder of 84 Lumber

WHEN A YOUNG JOE Hardy was working as a salesman in his family's jewelry store, he met a man he would remember for the rest of his life. The customer hailed from a small town called Eighty Four, Pennsylvania. Years later, Hardy had forgotten the man's name, but that of the town stuck with him.

When Hardy decided to open his own lumber yard, the name Eighty Four still resonated with him. Hardy made Eighty Four, Pennsylvania, his headquarters and named his company 84 Lumber.

Over the next half-century, 84 Lumber grew and prospered. From a single yard in Pennsylvania, Hardy established a chain of lumber yards across the United States. He lived the American dream, engineering success with his own wit and daring. Through innovation, perseverance, and an unwavering conviction that nothing is impossible, Hardy built a billion-dollar empire and his fortune.

But even as his holdings grew exponentially, Hardy never forgot the lessons he had learned at the start of his career. The more he prospered, the more interest he took in charitable projects and the welfare of his workers. As a result, his influence has spread across the country and around the world, and he continues to leave an indelible impression on all who meet him.

Turbulent Times

Joseph Alexander Hardy III began life in 1923 in the rolling hills of Pittsburgh. He was the first of three boys born to Norman "Bart" Hardy, who came from a well-to-do family, and Kathryn Stevenson Hardy, a bricklayer's daughter. Despite the differences in their social status, the two eloped and were married in Wellsburg, West Virginia.[1] At first, many of their acquaintances refused to recognize their marriage socially, but by the time their first son was born, the couple was living happily in Pittsburgh's East End.

Hardy was born during an exciting but turbulent time for the United States and for Pittsburgh in particular. World War I was over, the Roaring Twenties were in full swing, and jazz clubs and dance halls abounded. Pittsburgh was a prosperous city, and jobs were plentiful as the region's steel industry boomed. The state of perpetual twilight from the clouds of pollution from the steel mills was accepted by most residents as a sign that the local

Mr. and Mrs. Ellsworth Phillips, shown here about 1900, owned the grocery store in the area that would become Upper St. Clair, Pennsylvania, the Pittsburgh suburb where Joe Hardy grew up. *(Photo courtesy of Upper St. Clair Historical Society)*

industries were productive and the economic out-look was favorable.

While the era was defined by unprecedented financial success and an overall carefree spirit, the 1920s also brought a notable change in the U.S. Constitution. In 1920, the 18th Amendment, ban-ning the sale, production, and transport of alcohol, took effect. Prohibition was especially significant in Pittsburgh, whose bars and saloons outnumbered those of cities of similar size and quenched the thirst of the city's vast labor force.[2]

Hardworking Pittsburghers had little use for the new law.[3] Speakeasies sprang up around the city, and rumrunners made sure there was a steady supply of bootleg liquor.[4] A year after Prohibition was introduced, Pittsburgh was still known to some as "the wettest spot in the United States."[5] After two Prohibition agents tried and failed to dry out the city, local police and bootleggers collaborated to keep the city's stills and speakeasies operational,[6] and Pittsburgh became a major center of anti-Prohibition efforts.[7]

During the same time, the ethnic make-up of the city was also evolving. Pittsburgh's mills and factories lured thousands of immigrants, particularly from Russia, the Ukraine, and Eastern Europe, and the city became a patchwork of ethnic neighborhoods in which the residents preserved the traditions of their home countries. In 1921, however, Congress passed a law that greatly reduced the number of immigrants who could enter the United States from Europe.[8] This ended the great influx of immigrants into the Steel City, and gradually the ethnic groups began to blend into a more homogeneous, pan-American culture.[9]

But like every American born during the 1920s, Joe Hardy's formative years were defined by the Great Depression. In the years preceding the market crash of 1929, Pittsburgh's industries were boom-ing,[10] and local companies such as U.S. Steel and Westinghouse commanded staggering prices on the stock market up until the day of the crash.[11]

This view of Clifton, Pennsylvania, in the suburbs south of Pittsburgh, shows the town's blacksmith shop. Clifton would later become Upper St. Clair. *(Photo courtesy of Upper St. Clair Historical Society)*

Joe Hardy attended elementary school at the Clifton School House near his home, but he credited his mother, Kathryn Hardy, with instilling the values of family, responsibility, and self-reliance that he carried with him for the rest of his life. *(Photo courtesy of Upper St. Clair Historical Society)*

In the aftermath, however, Pittsburgh, like the rest of the United States, was soon struggling to make ends meet. One of many national "hunger marches," comprised of unemployed people, traveled from Pittsburgh to Washington, D.C., to appeal to the federal government for aid.[12] The 15,000-person march was just one sign of a changing city.[13] In 1932, the historically Republican voters of Pittsburgh overwhelmingly chose Democrat Franklin Delano Roosevelt as the next president of the United States.[14]

These social, economic, and cultural changes stirring during Joe Hardy's childhood would influence his business decisions throughout his life.

During this period, the Hardy family had welcomed a second son, Norman, in 1927, and their third child, Robert, later called Bob by his friends, followed two years later. After Bob was born, the family moved from Pittsburgh's East End to Upper St. Clair, a suburban neighborhood a few miles south of the city. They would remain there, in the Brookside Farms community, until Joe Hardy's high school years.

Early Lessons

Hardy received his early education in the Clifton School House near his home,[15] but the most significant influence on his life was his mother, Kathryn Hardy.

Kathryn Hardy, or Ma Hardy as her children referred to her, was a tough, self-reliant woman who kept her household running smoothly while her husband worked in downtown Pittsburgh. Her children recalled that their house was a gracious one, where friends were always welcome to visit and often invited to stay for supper.

Kathryn Hardy loved to cook and specialized in traditional meat-and-potatoes meals, as well as pies and cakes. She also made a direct contribution to the family dinner table—and the family finances—with her impressive vegetable garden. Long before victory gardens became popular during the Second World War, Kathryn Hardy tended an acre of garden space behind her house.[16] Whatever produce the Hardy family did not need, her children sold to neighbors.

As he grew up, Joe Hardy was closer to his mother than to anyone else. Those who knew the two of them said that they were cut from the same cloth, much more similar in manner and outlook than Hardy and his father. Kathryn Hardy was

Washington Road ran through Clifton, Pennsylvania. The Hardys lived in the area until a young Joe Hardy insisted they move to nearby Mt. Lebanon so he could live closer to Mt. Lebanon High School. *(Photo courtesy of Upper St. Clair Historical Society)*

known as the family disciplinarian, the voice of authority in the household.[17] Ma Hardy impressed upon Joe from an early age that he was responsible for the well-being of his younger brothers, and more than once Joe received a whipping for letting his little brother Bob wander off and get into trouble. He said it was a lesson well worth learning:

"That type of training just permeated my whole life," Hardy said. "I had to take care of people. ... Not only the family. This attitude just permeated my whole being and my whole living."[18]

In addition to teaching Joe to look out for others, his mother also instilled a sense of self-respect that started Joe on the path that would lead to his eventual success in the lumber industry. Hardy remembered some of the talks that he had with his mother which demonstrated her fierce love for him, as well as her impressive wisdom:

I don't think she graduated from high school, my mother, but if I would mess around with some jerks,

whatever you'd call them today, she'd say, "What are you fooling around with those people for?"

And I said, "Gee, Mom, they're a lot of fun. They're fun, fun, fun."

She said "Knock it off. You're something special, and you're going to amount to something."[19]

Joe Hardy emulated his mother's communication style of frankness, tough love, and no-nonsense interaction with everyone he met. It was an attitude that would serve him well in the business world.

His father, by contrast, was a quiet, easygoing man who spent his days at the family jewelry store, Hardy and Hayes, in downtown Pittsburgh. He was a respected figure in the community and doted on his three children.

"Well, he thought his sons were just perfect, and he was not the disciplinarian at all. But he was a fine, upstanding man," recalled Bob Hardy, his youngest son.[20]

His sons said that Bart Hardy never heard much about any sibling squabbles that went on in the Hardy household in his absence, as Kathryn Hardy was more than capable of making her three growing boys toe the line.

"She ruled the roost as far as the kids went," Bob Hardy said. "We were smart enough to know not to try to bypass her."[21]

On the rare occasions that Bart Hardy was called upon to discipline his sons, the situation would take on an almost comical tone, especially when Ma Hardy told him to use his razor strap. Bob Hardy recalled, "Mom would say, 'Get that razor strap out. [The boys] did this or that.' He'd go in the room, and he would pretend he would hit you or something. He wouldn't touch you."[22]

The boys, happy to protect their father's secret, screamed and cried on cue in order to convince their mother that they were being properly punished.

"He would never let on, and you'd better never let on," Bob Hardy said.[23]

Although Bart Hardy spent most of the day at work, he too passed valuable lessons along to his sons. The patrons of the jewelry store in which he worked were members of Pittsburgh's high society and were demanding customers. Joe Hardy learned from his father early on how to create an instant rapport with people and how to engender a sense of teamwork between client and customer.

Business Basics

The jewelry store, Hardy and Hayes, was a family business that also employed Joe Hardy's uncle, Paul Hardy.

Founded in 1887 by Joe Hardy's grandfather, Joseph Alexander Hardy I, Hardy and Hayes was a venerable Pittsburgh institution that Joseph Hardy I built from the ground up. Grandpa Hardy had begun his career in the jewelry business as a low-level clerk at a store called Wattles,[24] and over the years he worked his way up through the ranks, eventually opening his own store.

Hayes was an early partner who left the business soon after it started, but the name remains unchanged to this day, as Hardy and Hayes still serves the Pittsburgh area.

In its original location on Wood and Oliver streets in downtown Pittsburgh, the four-story Hardy and Hayes building contained several showrooms and offices.[25] The store, which employed about 40 people, was one of the most prestigious jewelry establishments in town. Several members of the Hardy family, including Joe Hardy's father, uncle, brothers, as well as Joe himself, would work at the store over the 100 years that it was family-owned.

In addition to creating his own success, Grandpa Hardy was one of Joe Hardy's early models of the entrepreneurial spirit. Having started his career as a simple errand boy, Joseph Hardy I had earned millions of dollars from his jewelry business and real estate investments by the time he died in 1934.[26]

One reason for the store's success was Grandpa Hardy's special expertise in pearls. These days, most of the pearls used to make fine jewelry are "cultured," meaning they are created by injecting mother-of-pearl beads into oysters so that those oysters will produce pearls around the beads. In the 1920s and '30s, however, the only pearls available were those created by natural ocean conditions.

As such, high-quality pearls were extremely valuable. Grandpa Hardy was a nationally consulted authority on the classification, grading, and valuation of fine pearls, and it was this specialized skill that helped build Hardy and Hayes into a profitable family business.

Throughout the years, many of Pittsburgh's most prominent families frequented the store. Magnates such as the Mellons in banking, the Fricks in coke,

The Drake streetcar stop in Upper St. Clair, Pennsylvania, was part of a route that ran all the way to Washington, Pennsylvania, close to what would eventually become 84 Lumber headquarters. *(Photo courtesy of Upper St. Clair Historical Society)*

and the Carnegies in steel visited the store for their jewelry purchases.[27] In fact, Joe Hardy claimed that one of his Uncle Paul's side interests in working at the store was trying to set up romances between his daughter and the city's young millionaires![28]

Paul would also be an important presence in Joe Hardy's life and in the history of the family business, as he eventually advocated selling the jewelry store after Grandpa Hardy's death.[29] Paul Hardy had an aristocratic sensibility, and occasionally took Joe Hardy to the Duquesne Club, one of Pittsburgh's most exclusive private clubs.[30] Here again, Joe Hardy

had the opportunity to mix with Pittsburgh's elite and learn the ways of the well-to-do.

Although the jewelry store was very successful, at times Grandpa Hardy's strong religious beliefs and his hard-nosed business sense came into conflict. For example, in the 1930s, "blue laws" prohibited most stores from opening on Sundays, a decree with which Grandpa Hardy heartily agreed.[31] Once, however, when Grandpa Hardy was away for the weekend, his son Paul placed an ad for the jewelry store in the Sunday paper. When Grandpa Hardy returned and heard about the ad he was initially furious and berated his son. Finally, however, his curiosity got the better of him.

"How was business Monday?" he asked. "Best Monday we ever had," Paul replied. Grandpa Hardy responded with a simple, "Oh," and was content to let the matter rest at that.[32]

As Joe Hardy grew up, the time he spent in his grandfather's store would teach him many valuable lessons. Hardy's curiosity led him to explore all aspects of the business, and he spent time in the accounting department, as well as on the sales floor.

The Hardy grandparents were also an important source of religious influence. Joe, Norman, and Bob Hardy sometimes attended Presbyterian church services on Sunday. When they didn't, they often spent Sundays at their paternal grandparents' East End home. Bob Hardy recalled that because of his grandfather's strict religious sensibilities, the boys were not allowed to go to the cinema on Sundays because it would require the theater staff to work on the Lord's Day.[33]

Lasting Relationships

Although they did not have such a large financial impact on his life, Joe Hardy's maternal grandparents were also very important to his development. "Pop" Stevenson, Kathryn Hardy's father, was a bricklayer. During Joe Hardy's childhood years, Pop was often out of work,[34] due in part to the dismal economic climate in 1930s America.

As a result, Joe Hardy spent more time with his Grandpa Stevenson than he did with his perpetually busy Grandpa Hardy. While Grandpa Hardy was working nonstop at Hardy and Hayes, Grandpa Stevenson had time to spend with Joe Hardy, either exploring the city or working in the vineyard that Stevenson kept behind his house.[35] As the years went by, Grandpa Stevenson would also help Joe Hardy with some early building projects, and the two became very close.

While family was the most important social influence on Joe Hardy's young life, he also met during these formative years someone who would be one of his closest friends throughout his life. Although Joe Hardy was confident and outgoing from childhood and had many friends, none would have as lasting an effect on his life as Edward Ryan.

Ryan lived a few houses down from the Hardys, and as the boys grew they became fast friends. Although they sometimes encouraged each other to create mischief, the boys had a mostly fruitful friendship that would eventually lead them into a business partnership. Ryan's father had to work delivering newspapers during the Depression, but afterwards he began a construction company.[36]

Ed Ryan would follow in his father's footsteps, and this would be a crucial influence on Joe Hardy's decision to enter the lumber business. The boys would go on to spend their high school and college years together and survive service in World War II.

Thus the people and places that surrounded Joe Hardy's early life left their mark. His father and mother taught him the social skills that would enable him to charm his way through many a difficult business venture. The close relationship that he developed with his brothers growing up in Pittsburgh would last throughout their lives and provide an invaluable support system once the three went into business together.

The fact that Joe Hardy grew up during the Great Depression may explain why, after he became a businessman and even after he achieved unqualified financial success, he was still famous for his strict thrift. But beyond all these influences, there was also an irrepressible spirit in Joe Hardy to create something of worth in the world around him, and as Hardy entered young adulthood, this quality began to shine.

In the world at large, the Great Depression was drawing to a close, and World War II was looming on the horizon. Pittsburgh would once again become a thriving center of industry as the steel mills roared into life to provide metal for the warplanes and ships.[37] Joe Hardy would have an important role to play in the region's economy and would demonstrate from high school onward an incredible toughness and ingenuity that would serve him well throughout his life.

Whether in school, the military, or the business world, Joe Hardy was well-known and well-liked by his colleagues. Fellow Shadyside Academy student Dale Armstrong remembered Hardy as "a young man who knew where he was going and had the wherewithal, convincing all of us he would get there. And more important, we wanted him to."

CHAPTER TWO

STARTING OUT

I told him, "Go out and do your thing." He said, "But I don't know any-thing." I said, "Sure you do. You know a lot of things, and you can do anything you make up your mind to do."

—Ed Ryan, former business partner and
lifelong friend of Joe Hardy

JOE HARDY BEGAN TO DISTIN-guish himself as a noteworthy young man both to his teachers and to his peers. When Hardy was ready to enter high school, Upper St. Clair, where his family lived, had no high school of its own,[1] so students from the area rode the bus to nearby Mt. Lebanon High School. Hardy decided that he would rather live in Mt. Lebanon and set about persuading his family to move.[2] Eventually he won his mother over, and once she made up her mind, the matter was decided.[3] The Hardy family moved to Mt. Lebanon.

All three of the Hardy boys would go on to attend Mt. Lebanon High, and all three would excel in sports. Both Bob and Norman Hardy played on the Mt. Lebanon High basketball team,[4] Norman participated in wrestling, and Bob was a boxer during his high school years.[5] The brothers sometimes sparred at home, although these contests gener-ally involved only Bob and Norman.[6]

But it was Joe Hardy, as the oldest brother, who was the standard bearer for the family in the world of high school sports. As a member of the Mt. Lebanon High Blue Devils football team, Hardy remembered joining his teammates for a couple of months before the school year began at a training retreat held on an Ohio farm owned by a teammate's father.[7] Hardy recalled that the training session helped to develop strong bonds among the players, who were soon fast friends on and off the field.[8]

When the football season began, Hardy played guard and was always try-ing to gain weight so that he could be an even more intimidating presence on the gridiron.[9] Hardy's power and tenacity on the football field made him an integral member of the team. Furthermore, the sense of closeness the team developed during pre-season training paid off. In Hardy's senior year, the Blue Devils, led by coach Henry Leucht, were unde-feated the entire season.[10] Hardy took away a busi-ness lesson from the experience and later used this same bonding technique to foster camaraderie and healthy competition among his top managers.

In addition to his football glory, Hardy also excelled in wrestling. He participated in many matches throughout his high school years and developed a reputation as a fierce, aggressive, and formidable competitor.

It was not only in sports that Hardy distin-guished himself. He was a generally well-liked and popular student, and was even voted "best-looking boy" in his high school class.[11] Friends who knew

---

Ed Ryan, whose family lived a few doors down from the Hardys when the boys were growing up, was one of Joe Hardy's best friends throughout his life. Ryan was instrumental in Hardy's decision to go into the lumber business, and years later, Hardy said Ryan was the only business partner he would ever have.

him at the time say that he was always popular with the girls, although this sometimes caused problems for him, Bob Hardy recalled.

There was a car repair place down in Bridgeville, which is a neighbor community to Mt. Lebanon, and I remember driving by it with my Mother and Dad, and the car repair man, body man, looked out ... and he waved at my mother. My Dad said "Gee, do you know him?" Well, Joe wasn't the greatest driver in the world as a young driver, and he'd be waving at the girls ... and bump into something, and Mother would have to take the car down there to have it fixed before Dad got home. Even though she was a tough one, she wanted to make sure everything was all right before our Dad got home.[12]

Deepening Bonds

Although Joe Hardy may have been popular with the girls at school, one particular young woman commanded his attention. Dorothy Pierce, known to her friends as Dottie, was something of a celebrity at Mt. Lebanon High because she arrived at school every day in a chauffeur-driven car.[13]

Her father, Robbins Pierce, was a vice president of the Atlantic and Pacific Tea Company, better known as the A&P grocery stores.[14] This company was one of the first in America to introduce the immensely successful idea of local chain grocery stores. As a result, even during the Depression years, the Pierce family, which also included Dottie's mother, Marguerite, and sister, Jane, was quite wealthy.[15]

Left: Hardy, fourth from the right in the second row, was a fierce wrestling opponent at Mt. Lebanon High School and later at Shadyside Academy. While at Shadyside, Hardy broke his jaw during a match but later continued to wrestle with his mouth wired shut.

Below: During Hardy's senior year, the Mt. Lebanon High Blue Devils football team was undefeated. Hardy can be seen in the front row, third from right, in this team photo.

Left top: Joe Hardy married his high school sweetheart, Dottie Pierce, who commanded attention at Mt. Lebanon High when she was driven to school by a chauffeur.

Left bottom: Ed Ryan married Dottie Pierce's best friend, Ann Chastaine.

Below: After graduating from high school, Joe Hardy spent a year at Shadyside Academy, a private school in the Pittsburgh suburbs where he met one of his closest friends, Peter Cameron. In this photo of Shadyside's class of 1942, Hardy is the third student from the right in the bottom row.

When Dottie reached high school, her family's affluence, as well as her charming personality, caught Joe Hardy's attention.[16] She and Hardy moved in the same circle of friends, and Dottie Pierce's best friend, Ann Chastaine, was dating Ed Ryan, Joe Hardy's friend since childhood.[17] Eventually, both young men married their high school sweethearts.

Although these were happy times for the boys, a terrible tragedy darkened Ed Ryan's high school years. When Ryan was 16, his father was killed in an auto accident while driving home from the Upper St. Clair Country Club.[18] In the Irish tradition, wakes were held following the funeral, and Joe Hardy was at his friend's side through it all.[19] Although the boys had been close for years, Hardy said that this experience deepened their attachment to one another. Thereafter, the boys were like brothers, and despite many changes of fortune and circumstance, their friendship persevered throughout their lives.

Standout Student

After graduating from Mt. Lebanon High School in 1941, Joe Hardy felt that he needed some additional preparation for college and spent a year at Shadyside Academy, a prestigious private school in the Pittsburgh suburbs. Shadyside was well-known for its sports program as well as its academics, and Hardy continued to play football and wrestle while at the academy.[20] Again, his aggressiveness set him apart from his fellow competitors.

During one wrestling match Hardy tackled an opponent so hard that both boys flew off the mat.[21] Hardy broke his jaw and had to have it wired shut for several weeks.[22] While Hardy drank his meals through a straw and his siblings joked that they

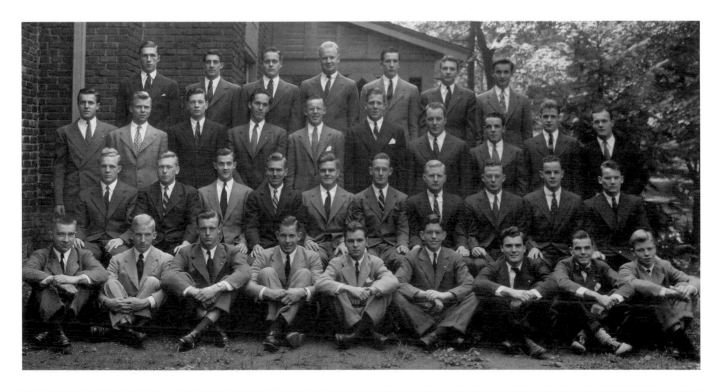

were enjoying their brother's sudden silence, Joe Hardy did not let his injury stand in the way of his activities.[23] He continued to wrestle, even with his broken jaw, and showed the Shadyside Academy sports spectators what true determination was all about.[24]

As at Mt. Lebanon High, Hardy was well-liked by his fellow students at Shadyside, and he was a well-known figure on the football field.[25] Looking back 40 years later, fellow Shadyside Academy student Dale Armstrong remembered Hardy's "sneaky sense of humor," "bright and friendly personality," and "total lack of fear."[26] He also recalled that Hardy was "a young man who knew where he was going and had the wherewithal, convincing all of us he would get there. And more important, we wanted him to."[27]

Among Hardy's many acquaintances at Shadyside, was a young man who would become one of his closest compatriots and a lifelong friend. Peter

Both Hardy, left, and his friend Ed Ryan attended Lehigh University in Bethlehem, Pennsylvania. Although Hardy was not a true academic, he wanted to prepare himself to face employers' scrutiny. He was intent on earning a degree, but World War II interrupted his education.

Cameron was two classes behind Joe Hardy at Shadyside Academy, but the two young men became good friends almost immediately.[28]

Cameron's family owned a bottling company that had been established in 1889[29] and was originally called Cameron Beverages. In 1916, the company secured a contract with the Coca-Cola company to bottle Coke,[30] and Cameron Coca-Cola soon became known nationwide. Pete Cameron and his two brothers went on to run the company, as had their father and grandfather before them,[31] and the business remained family-owned until it was sold in 1998.[32]

When Joe Hardy and Pete Cameron met in 1941, the Cameron bottling business was already well established, but the two young men did not have business on their minds.[33] Like Hardy, Cameron was very outgoing and sociable, and the two were natural and compatible friends. They spent many afternoons playing racquetball at the local YMCA,[34] and although they lost touch for a while when Hardy left to join the U.S. Army Air Forces, they resumed their friendship after the war.

When he began building 84 Lumber, Hardy often spent the night at Cameron's house, which was much closer to the lumberyard than Hardy's Upper St. Clair home.[35] This was also a convenient arrangement because, as Cameron's wife, Nan, recalled, both men liked to wake up at 4 A.M. to begin their day's work.[36]

A Close Call

After he left Shadyside Academy, Hardy went on to study engineering at Lehigh University in Bethlehem, Pennsylvania.[37] Ed Ryan also went to Lehigh, and the two young men continued their friendship.[38]

Although Hardy was not an academic at heart, he was determined to earn a college degree so that he would not find himself at a disadvantage when the time came to look for a job.[39] He had confidence in his ability to excel in whatever profession he chose, but he knew that many employers would not give him the benefit of the doubt. Although he sometimes had difficulty with his classes, he persevered and earned his education.

However, during Hardy's first year at Lehigh, it became clear that forces beyond his control would intervene. The Second World War was ravaging Europe, and there was an increasing need for America's young men on the battlefield. As the months progressed, Hardy realized that it was very likely that he would be drafted.[40] Rather than wait

Rather than waiting to be drafted, Joe Hardy, in the bottom row center, enlisted in the Army Air Forces during World War II. The military enrolled Hardy in several different specialist training programs before he finally completed a communications program.

for this to happen, he joined the Army Air Forces, as did Ed Ryan.[41]

The Air Forces put Joe Hardy through several training programs to prepare him for service.[42] However, as his brother Bob Hardy recalled, every time Joe Hardy was about to finish a program, the military decided that it had a greater need for specialists in a different area,[43] and Joe would then be sent to a different school to begin a new program.[44]

Eventually, he completed his training in communications and was sent to a military base in Florida to await his foreign assignment.[45] He ended up as a lieutenant in Guatemala and the Panama Canal, serving as an Air Forces radioman.[46] Meanwhile, Ed Ryan flew B-24 bombing missions, participating in the famous raids on the Ploesti oil fields in Romania, which served as Germany's major source of fuel.[47]

During one mission, Ryan experienced a close brush with death.

I was a navigator, and I was up in the nose of a B-24 with the nose gunner and the bombardier. The radioman who sat behind the copilot kept begging me to trade places with him. You weren't allowed to do that. I said, "Why?" He said, "I want to drop the bomb." So we trade places, and he's up in the

nose of the plane ... and he was so nervous and excited, his thumb hit, and our bombs went out before they were supposed to.... We got a direct hit in the nose of the plane. Blew the nose of the plane off, and all those guys were killed, and where I was supposed to be, I would have been killed, but I wasn't, but the plane was on fire, and it was out of control. Thank God he had gotten the bombs out before they were supposed to go out."

Ryan said having a parachute on his chest had interfered with his navigation work, and when the plane was hit, he had to scramble to find it.

The pilot said, "Abandon ship." I can't find the doggone parachute. Everybody gets out of the plane. The pilot says, "Ed, I said abandon ship." I said, "I can't find my parachute." The plane is on fire. Totally out of control. He said, "You've just been made captain of the ship." I'm the only one in this B-24, and it's going this way and this way and this way. I thought I was dead. I had no parachute,

and my God, I see that parachute flying by, and I grabbed it, and I catch it, and I snap it on.

Even after finding his parachute, Ryan's ordeal was far from over. On his way out of the plane, he hit his head and was knocked unconscious.

Well, thank God I was unconscious because when I came to ... I was on fire, and I was blind for four weeks, and I was paralyzed for four months.[48]

The New Pittsburgh

Back in Pittsburgh, Americans were experiencing the war in a completely different way than the

During World War II, Lt. Joe Hardy served as a radioman in the Army Air Forces, stationed in Guatemala and the Panama Canal. His good friend Ed Ryan flew B-24 bombers and participated in the Ploesti oil field raids in Romania.

young people on the front lines. The steel mills were working overtime. In fact, from December 9, 1941, when the front page headline of the *Pittsburgh Press* read "U.S. Declares War!," until the war ended in 1945, the Pittsburgh area mills produced 95 million ingot tons of steel.[49]

These resources were crucial to the United States and Allied war efforts. At the same time, however, the increased steel production added to the Smoky City's already staggering smog problem.[50] Streetlights burned at noon, and all of Pittsburgh's buildings were covered in a layer of black grime.

It was during the war years that a group of concerned citizens, rallied by *Pittsburgh Press* editor Edward Leech, City Health Director Ike Alexander, and City Councilman Abraham Wolk, began to formulate plans to clean up the city in the post-war period.[51] Banker Richard King Mellon of Pittsburgh's prominent Mellon family and future mayor of Pittsburgh David L. Lawrence soon joined the effort,[52] and the fight was on to make sure that the Pittsburgh that Joe Hardy and Ed Ryan came home to would be a very different one than the smoke-filled burgh that people across the nation had come to think of when they pictured the Steel City.

Thus, when Hardy and Ryan returned home they found a city that was remaking itself. Starting in 1946 after Lawrence was elected mayor, the city's Renaissance began. Strict smoke control ordinances were put in place, first for businesses and then for residences.[53]

Later, the area where the Monongahela, Allegheny, and Ohio rivers converge was restructured to become the Point, Pittsburgh's Golden Triangle. The area was initially filled with slums and run-down buildings, and it was a long, hard battle for city government officials to acquire property rights to it.[54] After they succeeded, however, new businesses moved in, and a section of land was developed into Point State Park. This park showcased historic Fort Pitt and would eventually include a breathtaking fountain at the confluence of the three rivers.

Elsewhere in town, a host of new buildings was constructed, including the U.S. Steel, Mellon Bank, and Alcoa Buildings. A Public Parking Authority and Urban Redevelopment Authority were also established.[55] Pittsburgh was growing and changing, making a fresh name for itself and heading in new directions. Joe Hardy knew that it was time for him to do the same.

Setting Up House

After returning from military service, Hardy married Dorothy Pierce, his girlfriend since high school, in 1943.

"They were the most handsome couple, Dottie and Joe, and she was a real beauty," recalled Betty Gottschalk, a close friend of Dottie Hardy for more than 50 years.

The young couple decided to buy a home in which to raise a family and chose a farmhouse that had once been owned by the Fifes, one of the prominent founding families of Upper St. Clair. The land where the Hardys' new home stood had been a homestead in the 1840s and had originally been purchased by the Fifes from the American Indians in the area.[56]

The Fife House, as it came to be called by Hardy and his friends, was purchased for $6,500 but needed a great deal of repair.[57] With the vision that would propel him through many projects over the years, Hardy recognized the potential in the old house and resolved to renovate the building and make it a home he could be proud of.

He had plenty of help. Though Ed Ryan would one day own one of the nation's largest home building companies, the Fife house was his first major construction project. Since returning from the war, Ryan had been working as a carpenter's assistant at the rate of $1.25 an hour,[58] and when Hardy bought his farmhouse, Ryan had more enthusiasm than expertise.

As Ryan and Hardy were rebuilding the house, Ryan recalled that he often knew exactly what needed to be done, but not how to do it,[59] and at times, Ryan's excitement for the project did more harm than good. Once, for example, Hardy left a stack of window panes inside the house that he wanted Ryan to install. When Ryan walked into the house, he was so eager to get to work that he didn't even see the windows and crashed through the entire pile.[60]

The two men also had help from Pop Stevenson, Joe Hardy's grandfather. In the style of many old farmhouses, the Fife house had a fireplace in almost every room, and all of them needed to be rebuilt.[61] Because Grandpa Stevenson was a bricklayer by trade, he was the ideal person for the job in many

Joe Hardy, third from left, is seen enjoying a drink and a cigar with several Army buddies, including Ed Ryan, center. In later years, Hardy would conduct many business meetings with a cigar dangling from his lips, although it was rarely lit.

ways. However, Hardy recalled that his grandfather and Ed Ryan sometimes locked horns over the way that the work should be completed.

"Ed would start at, say, 7 in the morning, and Pop would roll in there about 8," Hardy said. "Ed would be looking at his watch, you know, and Pop would say, 'OK, Ed, I know. I'm starting a little late, but I'm going to make up for it, and I'm going to quit early.' "[62]

The three men enjoyed working together, however, and eventually the home underwent a dramatic transformation. One of its most distinctive features was a barn next to the house. Hardy installed wall-to-wall red carpeting in the barn and converted it into a party room.[63] While most of their friends were still living in cramped apartments, Joe and Dottie Hardy were able to host festivities for all of their family and friends.

The Fife House also became the center for Hardy family reunions for decades, and the biggest party of the year was one thrown each Christmas Eve. The family would decorate a huge Christmas tree, and the children would line up at the top of the staircase to sing "The Twelve Days of Christmas."[64] Dottie

Hardy's grandchildren recalled that she especially loved these events, where she could play the hostess and welcome the people she loved into her home.[65]

In his typical fashion, Hardy quickly became a familiar presence in his new neighborhood. Former neighbor Newton Teichman recalled that when he decided to build his own home near Hardy's Fife House, Hardy often came by to "check up" on the construction work. Teichman said, "At that time Joe had an oversized raccoon coat which he lived in during his land inspection tours, and so I would see Joe coming across the tundra with the familiar cigar smoke coming out of the top of the mass of raccoon fur, and I knew I was up for inspection."[66]

Teichman also recalled Hardy's friendliness and civic-mindedness. Teichman once took refuge in the Hardy house during a snowstorm and ended up staying for two days, playing bridge with the family and having a wonderful time.[67] In addition to their personal relationships with their neighbors, the Hardys pitched in to shape the developing community around their home. Joe Hardy worked in the community garden, and Dottie Hardy campaigned to get the rough and rutted Fife Road repaired.[68]

The Hardys found out quickly that the large farmhouse had been a wise choice for their family. The couple's first child, Joseph Hardy IV, was born in 1947, and a second son, Paul, came along the following year. Three daughters were still to come.

Born Salesman

With a new home and a growing family to provide for, Joe Hardy knew he had to plan carefully for his future. He enrolled at the University of Pittsburgh, where he studied engineering.[69] But Hardy needed a way to support himself and his family while pursuing his studies. He earned some money by continuing in the Army Reserve on weekends, and he also went back to work at the Hardy and Hayes jewelry store.[70]

In addition to these traditional jobs, Joe Hardy was never without creative ways to supplement his income. The Fife property included a large parcel of land, containing a two-acre cornfield.[71] Hardy used to fill the trunk of his station wagon with ears of corn and drive around Mt. Lebanon with his brother Bob, selling corn door-to-door.[72] This brought in a few extra dollars to supplement the Hardy family income although Bob Hardy recalled that there were times when Joe's varied occupations came into conflict. He said that once, when they came to a house with their produce, Joe refused to make the sale.

"Joe said, 'You go sell to these people, I sold to them at the jewelry store today, and I don't want them to see me selling corn at night.' "[73]

At Hardy and Hayes, on the other hand, nothing could hold Joe Hardy back. He was studying gemology, eager as always to learn as much as pos-sible about the business in which he was involved. But Hardy demonstrated his true talent on the sales floor. Although he was one of the newer salesmen at the store, Hardy had a way with customers.

Shortly after starting work, he became Hardy and Hayes' top salesman. Hardy kept improving his sales record, until finally one day, his uncle Paul, one of the store's managers, invited Joe Hardy to lunch at the Duquesne Club.[74] This private gentlemen's club was frequented by all of Pittsburgh's most illustrious aristocrats, and as Hardy looked forward to the special appointment, he wondered whether he was going to receive a promotion or even stock in the family business.[75] When the meal began, however, he got quite a surprise. Hardy's uncle scolded him for his record sales, telling the young man that he was too aggressive.[76]

"He said, 'Boy, I don't know what you're doing, but do you realize you're selling as much as any five of those other guys are selling? Back off, boy.' "[77]

Hardy was stunned. He could not believe that his hard work was not only going unappreciated, but being criticized. Shortly after the conversation with his uncle, Joe Hardy decided that he could not continue to work at Hardy and Hayes. He needed an arena where he would be able to use his selling skills and be as aggressive as was necessary to make the sales. His friend Ed Ryan supported him in this decision. Ryan remembered a conversation he had with Hardy shortly after his fateful lunch at the Duquesne Club.

"I told him, 'Go out and do your thing.' He said, 'But I don't know anything.' I said, 'Sure you do. You know a lot of things, and you can do anything you make up your mind to do.' "[78]

That was a philosophy that Joe Hardy would live by for years to come. Although his father was crushed when he decided to leave the family jewelry business, he had made up his mind.[79] He left Hardy and Hayes and soon after entered the field in which he would ultimately make his legend and his fortune—the lumber industry.

Joe and Dottie Hardy, seen on their wedding day in 1943, had already started their family when Joe and his brothers established Green Hills Lumber. It soon became apparent that the business wouldn't be able to support the Hardy brothers, Ed Ryan, as well as their growing families.

CHAPTER THREE

LEARNING THE LUMBER BUSINESS

Hardy could turn a room into magnificent surroundings with his vision....
When I walked out of that first meeting [I thought], "Wow, this man is
sensational. He's going to be a real success, and so is his company."

—Helen Dolfi, Green Hills Lumber transcriptionist

ALTHOUGH HE HAD DECIDED TO leave Hardy and Hayes, Joe Hardy did not yet know where he was headed. Once again, his friend Ed Ryan would be instrumental in helping him keep on the path to success.

Ryan was running his own house-building company and convinced Hardy to start a lumberyard as a business partner.[1] Hardy would supply the lumber for Ryan's homebuilding business and for any additional customers the two could attract. Because the men would have their own lumber business, they would be able to acquire lumber for Ryan's projects at wholesale prices, thereby giving him a competitive edge.

Hardy found a building on McMurray Road, a main roadway outside Pittsburgh, to serve as the headquarters for his new endeavor.[2] The rent was just $50 a month, with a dirt lot for parking and lumber storage.[3] In 1948, Ed Ryan, Hardy, and Hardy's two brothers, Norman and Bob, each contributed $5,000 for start-up costs for the new business, which they named Green Hills Lumber.[4]

Once a location had been chosen, Hardy set to work organizing the business and getting it up and running. Initially, he had some competition for this responsibility. Ed Ryan's father-in-law, a military hero whom he and Hardy referred to only as Col. Chastaine, joined the new business as manager.

Chastaine was a devoutly religious man and had started his own church upon returning from World War II.[5] During the war, he had earned an impressive list of military honors and had been a prisoner of war in Japan.[6] Ryan said his father-in-law survived the infamous Bataan Death March on one banana a day, eating one-third of it for each meal.[7]

When Chastaine came to Green Hills Lumber, however, the skills that had served him so well in the military did not sit well with Joe Hardy. The new lumberyard had only a handful of employees and was a bare-bones operation, but both Hardy and Ryan recalled that Chastaine wanted to run the store like a military base, with extreme discipline and strict attention to protocol at every step.[8] Eventually it became clear that the partnership was unworkable, and Chastaine left Green Hills Lumber.

Bud and Helen Dolfi, seen here at 84 Lumber's "Roman Orgy" party in 1979, were long-time associates of Joe Hardy. Helen Dolfi, who typed the minutes for Green Hills Lumber board meetings, remembered that Hardy's enthusiasm for the business was contagious. After meetings, she usually couldn't sleep and spent the evening typing up her transcript notes.

Meeting Challenges

The other employee at the lumberyard was a young woman whom Hardy remembered only as Tessie. Tessie was the secretary and receptionist at Green Hills, and whatever her clerical qualifications, she had one very important skill that would be invaluable in the early days of Green Hills Lumber. Initially, when Ryan and the Hardy brothers had trouble earning enough money to pay their bills, it was usually Tessie who kept the creditors at bay. Hardy recalled:

We couldn't pay any bills. We literally would throw them in the air and pay maybe whatever we could. I said to [Tessie] one time with my brother, Norman ... "Tessie, what do you tell these bill collectors?" She looked at us ... and she said, "You know, I just play dumb." We rolled on the floor [laughing].[9]

Despite these early financial troubles, Hardy and Ryan charged full steam into the lumber business. Although they faced many challenges, they did have some help on their side. Toward the end of World War II, Hardy recalled that it was still difficult to obtain automobiles for business use.[10] Hardy and Ryan needed a truck to make their deliveries, however, if their business was to be successful.

Fortunately, Hardy's father-in-law used his clout as a vice president of A&P to get a vehicle for Green Hills Lumber.[11] Hardy also found another, older truck and started using the vehicles to deliver lumber.

There were some early lessons to be learned. Hardy was determined to get the most use possible out of his hard-to-find trucks, and so he loaded them with as much lumber as he could in order to speed his deliveries along. He would keep loading a truck with lumber until it was almost ready to tip over backwards, then speed off down the rough country roads. Ryan recalled one time when they had an especially heavy load of lumber. Ryan sat in the back with the lumber and a rope to hold the wood down, while Hardy drove.[12] As they made their way down Kelso Road near their Mount Lebanon neighborhood, Hardy hit a bump.[13] Both Ryan and the load of the lumber were pitched into the middle of the road.[14] Such challenges, however, only encouraged Hardy to come up with more ingenious ways to boost his business.

Robbins Pierce, Joe Hardy's father-in-law and a vice president of the Atlantic and Pacific Tea Company, contributed some of the start-up money for Green Hills Lumber. Pierce also used his clout at A&P to obtain a delivery truck for the new company.

In some ways, Hardy and Ryan's partnership was a key element in the success of Green Hills. The two men got along well, and even 50 years later Joe Hardy said that Ed Ryan was the only person he would ever want to be partners with.[15]

Ryan concurred. "Joe and I were like brothers, and we'd been through an awful lot," he said. "We could totally, totally trust each other. We never had to have anything in writing. ... His word was his bond. He could trust me, and I could trust him."[16]

According to Virginia "Ginny" Hackman, a close friend of the Hardys who had known Joe since high school, the men also shared a vision of where the lumber industry could take them. She recalled one conversation that took place during the 1950s:

They were sitting on our porch one evening, and Ed and Joe were talking about the future and talking about the baby boomers. ... Joe and Ed were saying [that] in about 20 to 22 years, these kids will be out of college, and they'll be looking for an afforable home. It was Ed saying, "I'm going to be the one to build the homes that these kids are going to buy, and Joe is going to supply the lumber." That's how far ahead their thinking was at that time.[17]

But the Hardy-Ryan partnership did cause some initial business problems for Green Hills because other builders did not appreciate the collaboration. Although Green Hills Lumber had some of the cheapest building supplies available in the area, contractors were often reluctant to buy from Hardy because of his connection with Ryan, another homebuilder.[18] They considered Ryan their competition and did not want to support any business that would put money in his pocket.[19] The irony of the situation was that Ryan was building only three or four houses a year,[20] while larger rivals were building dozens or hundreds in response to an enormous postwar demand for new housing.[21] Hardy and Ryan stuck together, but Hardy knew he would have to find novel ways to bring in customers and keep Green Hills Lumber afloat.

One solution was to begin selling plaster. At the time, plastering was a complicated operation that required bags of lime and heavy rock lath.[22] Most builders near Green Hills Lumber did not want to deal with the hassle of plastering, so they subcontracted to plasterers, who bought their own supplies.[23]

Hardy courted these plasterers as his new clientele and began ordering truckloads of plastering supplies. When the supplies arrived he had to go out and sell some of them immediately for cash so that he could pay the freight bill, which was due within 24 hours.[24] Afterwards, he would sell the rest of the supplies to whomever he could find willing to buy.

Hardy was willing to go to great lengths to gain and retain customers. Plasterers sometimes called him in the evening with job orders for the next day.[25] Hardy then worked until the early hours of the morning hauling plaster to job sites.[26] He recalled that Green Hills was always technically bankrupt, but he kept making deliveries, bringing in money and paying the bills, constantly staying just one step ahead of financial failure by constant motion.[27]

It was the first instance of what would become a catchphrase among 84 Lumber employees, "We lose a little on every sale, but we make it up in volume."[28]

A New Family Business

Hardy soon gained some help with the struggling business when his brother Norman returned from the army.

Dottie and Joe Hardy's first child, Joseph Alexander Hardy IV, was born in 1947. While her husband worked around the clock making deliveries for Green Hills Lumber and then building the 84 Lumber empire, Dottie took care of most of the household and child-rearing responsibilities for the family.

Norman Hardy came to work at Green Hills Lumber, and Ed Ryan recalled that Norman's sensible, low-key attitude provided the perfect balance to Joe Hardy and Ed Ryan's headlong enthusiasm.[29] Norman was quickly chosen as the company's salesman. His first day on the job at Green Hills, Norman surveyed the site and asked his brother Joe what his duties would be.[30]

Joe Hardy recalled:

I said, "Well, we have no sales. I want you to sell." He looks out at our half-acre, and we had maybe one little pile of lumber. He said, "Well, what will I sell?" I said, "You dumb kid, all around Pittsburgh, they have all these wholesalers and have everything you'd build a house with. That's what you sell." He said, "Well, what should I charge?" And I said, "We never got around to making a price list. Get anything you can." That was his orientation to be a salesman.[31]

Once he got started, however, Norman proved to be a stellar salesman. He developed an instant

---

Joe Hardy and his sons, Paul and Joe Jr., right, enjoy a rowboat ride on Lake Chautauqua with friends Dave and John Eaton. The Hardy family would soon grow to include three daughters—Robin, Kathy, and later, Maggie.

rapport with the subcontractors on job sites and earned their loyalty and appreciation.

Joe Hardy recalled that one of Norman's favorite tricks was to take a silver dollar with him to a work site and "accidentally" drop it while talking to a contractor.[32] Another tactic was to offer a particularly low price on a material that a certain builder needed a high volume of in order to get that builder to transfer all of his business to Green Hills.[33] Norman also was known to go beyond the requirements of business to help his customers when they were having financial or personal difficulties.[34]

Joe Hardy recalled that once Norman had gained his customers' loyalty, they would go to great lengths to make sure Green Hills Lumber got their repeat business:

He got into these different guys to the point where he'd come around on a job, and the subcontractor or whatever you'd call him would come up to him and say, "I wasn't here yesterday. Did Green Hills deliver this load?" My brother would say no. So then when the builder would come around, the subcontractor would run up and say, "I don't know where you're getting [these supplies], but I'm going to have to charge another $500 if you're going to continue to get this crappy, crappy lumber...." So the builder would say, "OK, I'll get that stuff from Green Hills." I mean [Norman] had

Joe Hardy holds a young Joe Jr., as he and his wife, Dottie, center, enjoy a Christmas celebration with family and friends. Strong family ties held the Hardy brothers together when rare disagreements arose at Green Hills Lumber.

that kind of a rapport and building a loyalty where the sub would say, "Don't worry about it, Norm. We'll take care of it."[35]

Even with Norman helping out, however, Green Hills still faced some difficulties. Almost all of its sales were done on credit, and many clients failed to pay their bills on time. Considering the fledgling company's already precarious financial situation, this created a lot of problems for the Hardys and Ryan.

It fell to Joe Hardy to visit builders who owed money and try to convince them to pay their bills. He tried many things, including waiting on debtors'

steps in the early hours of the morning so that he could talk to them when they left for work.[36] But Ed Ryan recalled that the most successful tactic that Hardy developed was to visit the builders at home on Saturday night, and remind them of their debts while their wives stood watching.[37]

Bill-collecting was not Hardy's only task. He also helped with sales and ran the Green Hills office. Throughout his life he would be a hard worker who was committed to his business, and his time at Green Hills was no exception. Hardy sometimes worked 24 hours straight making deliveries because he had only two trucks at his disposal.[38]

In 1955, the company got another helping hand when Bob Hardy left the military and came to work at Green Hills.[39] Bob was put in charge of the lumberyard, while Norman continued to head up sales and Joe Hardy ran the office.[40] Despite these job titles, the three brothers worked as a team on all aspects of the business.

ED RYAN FUELS FAMILY'S LOVE OF BUILDING

ED RYAN AND JOE HARDY MET DURING their childhood years and remained lifelong friends. Hardy's personal relationship and business partnership with Ryan were important driving forces behind the founding of Green Hills Lumber and later 84 Lumber. But after Ryan left Green Hills Lumber, he became a success in his own right with his homebuilding company, Ryan Homes.

The homebuilding tradition began with Ryan's father, also named Edward Ryan. On his wedding day in 1925, Edward Ryan Sr. promised his new bride that he would build a home for the two of them to live in.[1] Working nights and weekends, he began building a home on Rockwood Drive in Castle Shannon, Pennsylvania.[2] When the house was nearly completed, a man offered to buy it. After asking his wife's permission, Edward Ryan Sr. agreed to sell the house and promised to build her a new one.[3]

From this fortuitous beginning, Edward Ryan Sr. developed a reputation as a skilled home-builder. He began building homes for other people and soon established a business, E.J. Ryan

There were few arguments between them, and when the rare disagreement did surface, the Hardys' strong family ties brought them back together. Joe Hardy recalled one time when Bob and Norman had an argument at the lumberyard. Bob left the site and went back to Mount Lebanon, planning to go to the University of Pittsburgh job center and find a new job immediately.[41] On his way, however, he stopped at his mother's house for lunch. When he finished eating, Kathryn Hardy took her son to task

Homes.[4] However, the business endeavor came to an abrupt end when Ed Ryan Sr. was killed in a tragic car accident.[5]

After his death, the Ryan homebuilding company remained dormant for several years.[6] The Ryan family was in desperate financial straits but managed to hold onto the deeds to some of the company's properties.[7] When Ed Ryan Jr. returned from serving in World War II, his mother urged him to revive the business, and in 1947,[8] he did so with the help of his two brothers.[9] The new construction venture was incorporated under the name Edward M. Ryan Inc.[10]

Throughout the 1950s, the business grew in response to the postwar demand for housing and expanded from its home base in the Pittsburgh area to serve other regions in Pennsylvania.[11] In 1961, the company name was changed to Ryan Homes Inc.,[12] and during the 1960s, Ed Ryan expanded the company's markets even further to serve Harrisburg, Pennsylvania; Cleveland, Ohio; Columbus, Ohio; and Rochester, New York.[13]

As the 1960s progressed, Ryan began to investigate new products and services that would make the company even more successful. In order to gain greater control over the entire homebuilding process, Ryan Homes established its own lumberyards and manufacturing plants.[14] It also became involved in subdivision planning, and in 1966 the company started a panelization project.[15]

The 1970s brought more expansion when Ryan Homes became involved with inner-city construction and planned unit development.[16] Its product lines were upgraded in 1976 to appeal to higher-budget customers,[17] and new markets were established in Louisville, Kentucky, and Indianapolis, Indiana, as well as Virginia, Maryland, Georgia, North Carolina, Florida, and other areas.[18]

In 1986, Ryan Homes was acquired by NVHomes L.P., and the company name was changed to NVRyan L.P.[19] These days, under the NVR umbrella, Ryan Homes also provides home financing.[20] The company now builds everything from single-family homes to condominiums in New York, New Jersey, Pennsylvania, Delaware, Ohio, North Carolina, South Carolina, Maryland, Virginia, and West Virginia.[21]

To date, the company that Ed Ryan founded has constructed more than 200,000 homes[22] and has received high customer satisfaction ratings in markets across the United States.[23]

Although Ed Ryan has retired from the business, the family interest in building homes has continued. Both of his brothers established their own homebuilding companies, and several of their children also went on to work in the industry or started construction companies of their own.[24] One of them, Ed Ryan's nephew William J. Ryan started Ryan Building Group in 1992.[25]

When asked why so many members of his family chose to pursue a career in the homebuilding industry, he said that because his grandfather had died at a relatively young age, Ed Ryan Jr. had truly set the course for generations to come.

"I think that a lot of it has to do with just the dominant force that Ed Ryan was for all the brothers, basically taking the family from the poverty level to being very, very successful," William Ryan said. "Ryan Homes, as an example of what the building industry can do for you economically, was a driving factor for many of us. Ed Ryan has a dominant style and did a lot of innovative things in the business ... and the family has learned from that."[26]

Thanks to a promise by Ed Ryan Sr. and the dedication of his son Ed Ryan Jr., the Ryan family companies continue to thrive, building thousands more homes each year.

for arguing with his brother and ordered him back to the lumberyard,[42] and the three brothers were soon working side-by-side again.

For the most part, though, the business relationship between the Hardy brothers was a successful one, and early employees recalled the great camaraderie that existed between them.

Donna Criss, who was known to the Hardy brothers by her maiden name of Donna Verno, began working in 1955 as a secretary for Green

Hills.[43] She was still in high school at the time and worked after school and on Saturdays.[44] Criss recalled that despite the fact that the three brothers worked together every day, they maintained a great deal of affection for one another.

"When Norman or Bob would walk in that door, you would think Joe hadn't seen them for months, and they saw each other every day," she said. "It was like, 'Hi, how are you doing?' They loved each other."[45]

An Eye for Talent

Donna Criss became an important part of the Green Hills team and stayed with the company for several years. She said there was a general atmosphere of friendliness and acceptance that pervaded the Green Hills lumberyard.

When she started work at the company, she knew nothing about lumber and remembered Norman Hardy taking her on a tour of the warehouse to teach her to recognize different types of supplies.[46] She also remembered Joe Hardy as someone who always made her and the other employees feel important and respected.[47] Criss eventually went to work for one of Green Hills' subcontractors but maintained her connections to the company, and her daughter-in-law later worked for 84 Lumber.[48]

Like Criss, many early employees developed life-long associations with Joe Hardy's lumber business. As the years went by and sales increased, Green Hills' workforce grew. The company sometimes acquired employees in a haphazard way, but Joe Hardy's colleagues all agreed that he had an eye for talent. Both at Green Hills Lumber and in later years, he was often able to identify people who would spend their entire lives working for his company.

One of those people was Bud Dolfi, a homebuilder in Washington County, Pennsylvania, in the early 1950s who was in need of inexpensive lumber.[49] He heard about Green Hills Lumber and started buying his supplies from Joe Hardy. Soon he was using his truck to do odd jobs for Green Hills, hauling sand, mortar, and other supplies.[50]

One day, when Dolfi came to pick up a load of gravel from the lumberyard, he found the parking lot filled with customers.[51] One of them asked Dolfi for advice, and before Dolfi knew it he had spent his evening selling lumber.[52] Afterward, Hardy invited Dolfi to come to work for the company.[53] Dolfi agreed and ended up working not only at Green Hills but at its successor, 84 Lumber, for 47 years.[54]

Even after retiring in the 1980s, he continued to do consulting work for 84 Lumber for another 20 years and was a model of the loyalty that is common among the company's employees.[55]

Bud Dolfi's wife, Helen, also became involved with the lumber business through Hardy. When she was working toward a college degree and needed some extra money to supplement her income,[56] Helen

Opposite: Joe Hardy's parents, Kathryn and Norman "Bart" Hardy, wish their son, Bob, and new daughter-in-law, Mary, well on their wedding day. Hardy said his father was disappointed when he chose to leave the family jewelry store, Hardy and Hayes, but he soon established Green Hills Lumber with his two brothers as partners. *(Photo by The Brookner Studio, Pittsburgh, Pa.)*

Right: Bud Dolfi, seen here in a 1979 grand opening ad for 84 Lumber, was one of several employees identified early on as someone who would spend his life working for the company.

Dolfi began taking and transcribing minutes for the Green Hills Lumber board meetings. She recalled how they showcased the dynamism and enthusiasm of Joe Hardy and of the young company as a whole.

I wasn't there long... [before] the room became an arena of... motivational techniques, determination, and vision. Hardy could turn a room into magnificent surroundings with his vision. ...[57] *When I walked out of that first meeting [I thought], "Wow, this man is sensational. He's going to be a real success, and so is his company."*[58]

Helen Dolfi said that even after she left the meetings and returned home, the charged and energetic atmosphere of the board room affected her so much

that she usually spent the rest of the evening typing up her transcript notes.[59]

Willis Able, who later became the first manager of an 84 Lumber store, also came to work for Green Hills Lumber by unusual means. Able recalled:

I was laying the cement block on the foundation of my home, and [Joe] stopped and wanted to know if he could sell me the lumber to build my house, and I told him, "No, I'm working at Atlas Lumber Supply Company in Castle Shannon, and I already bought my lumber there because they gave me a discount." He says, "Yeah, but they're going out of business." I say, "I know they are." He said, "Well, what did you do there?" and I told him, "You know, I was a carpenter. We built all types of stairs and windows and doors and all things like that." He said, "Why don't you come to work for me?" and so I went to work for Joe in 1953.[60]

Inspiration Strikes

Along the way, Green Hills Lumber's financial prospects began to improve. Although the company still experienced difficulties in collecting bills, it had developed a more steady clientele.

The three Hardy brothers had put their skills to good use and had utilized their talents to make the business a success. Ed Ryan was also building more homes with Green Hills-supplied lumber, which also helped stabilize the company's finances.

But Joe Hardy had his doubts about the business. He was always looking to the future, and he could see problems on the horizon. How, he wondered, would Green Hills be able to support himself, his two brothers, Ryan, and their growing families in the years to come?

Since establishing Green Hills Lumber, Hardy's family had expanded. In addition to his two sons, Joe (who came to be known as Joe Jr.) and Paul, Hardy had been blessed with two daughters—Robin, who

Joe Hardy tried his hand at several business ventures, including prefabricated homes and real estate, but those projects didn't provide him with the opportunities he wanted. When he stumbled upon a cash-and-carry lumberyard on his way home from a business trip, he knew he'd found his life's work.

Joe Hardy was inspired to start a cash-and-carry lumber business on his way home from visiting his friend and former neighbor William "Bink" Conover, shown here in 1973, in Chicago.

was born in 1950, and Kathy, who joined the family in 1953. Though Dottie Hardy handled most of the day-to-day responsibilities of raising the children while her husband worked, Joe Hardy realized that his growing family, as well as those of the other partners, would soon need more financial support.

In 1955, Joe Hardy left Green Hills Lumber to experiment with other projects,[61] one of which was investing in prefabricated homes.[62] Although these home-building packages would later become a profitable focus for 84 Lumber, Hardy's initial interest was short-lived.

Hardy also tried his hand at selling real estate,[63] which provided him with skills that would eventually come in handy when he had to acquire new 84 Lumber building sites. Yet neither the prefabricated homes nor the real estate ventures really captured Hardy's imagination or seemed able to provide him with the growth and challenges he wanted.

Everything changed when Hardy visited his friend William Conover. Conover, known to his friends as "Bink," had been one of Hardy's neighbors in 1954, and worked as the assistant manager of an insurance company.[64] For a while he did some delivery work for Green Hills Lumber to earn extra money,[65] but eventually Conover moved to the Chicago area.[66]

He and Hardy met up one night when Hardy was in Chicago for a business meeting and could not find a place to stay.[67] As Hardy drove back to Pittsburgh the next day, he passed a lumber store called Wickes Cash and Carry.[68] The store was based on the concept, fairly new to the lumber industry, that all orders had to be paid for at the time of purchase, rather than being bought on credit.

Hardy immediately saw the potential of the idea. All his problems with trying to collect past-due bills would be eliminated, and overhead costs would be kept to a minimum. When Hardy arrived back in Pittsburgh, he told Ryan and his brothers that he planned to open his own cash-and-carry lumberyard.

Ryan was skeptical. "If [your clients] can't pay their bills in three months, how are you going to sell for cash?" Ryan wondered.[69] But Hardy believed that cash-and-carry was the idea that would set him on the road to business success. The partners sold Green Hills Lumber to a contractor,[70] and Hardy excitedly began making plans for what would become his life's work.

From the beginning, 84 Lumber was dedicated to the principle of "cash and carry." Because all orders were paid for at the time of purchase, the company always had the money to pay the lumber mills. This system also helped 84 Lumber achieve its goal of low prices and fast inventory turnover.

CHAPTER FOUR

84 LUMBER IS BORN

When I was in the jewelry store selling part-time, I remembered a guy that said he was from Eighty Four, Pennsylvania, and for some reason, Eighty Four stuck in my mind. Eighty Four, I thought it was a cryptic name, a cool name, a clean name.

—Joe Hardy, founder of 84 Lumber

ONCE JOE HARDY HAD DECIDED what his new business would be, he wasted no time in setting it up. His first task was to find a location for his proposed cash-and-carry lumberyard. The site selection process began with Hardy's recollection of a chance encounter he'd had seven years earlier.

"When I was in the jewelry store selling part-time, I remembered a guy that said he was from Eighty Four, Pennsylvania, and for some reason, Eighty Four stuck in my mind," he said. "Eighty Four. I thought it was a cryptic name, a cool name, a clean name. So for some reason, I don't know what it was, it steered me out to come to Eighty Four."[1]

Hardy traveled to the small town, nestled in the rolling countryside of Pennsylvania's Washington County, a sparsely populated area comprised primarily of farmland. Hardy set to work looking for the perfect plot of land on which to build his lumberyard and settled on a five-acre triangle of land that was adjacent to a larger farm.[2] When he went to speak to the owner about buying the property, the farmer told Hardy that the land would not be within his price range.

Hardy recalled, "I said, 'Yeah, well if you ever did sell it, what would you ask?' [He said,] 'I want $6,000.' I said, 'Sold.' So he wouldn't back out for some reason."[3]

Effective Strategies

After he had secured the land, Hardy still needed to obtain financing for his new venture. He calculated that he would need a $25,000 line of credit and settled on Union National Bank in Pittsburgh as the lending institution.[4]

But Hardy did not simply walk into the bank office and ask for a loan. The money was crucial to his proposed business, and he planned out his loan meeting as though he were devising a strategy for battle. Hardy found out everything he could about the bank and its employees and settled on a man named Willard Perry, who was second-in-command at the bank, as the man to ask for the money.[5]

Before Joe Hardy approached Perry, he took some advice from his brother Norman.

"[Norman would] always figure out the idiosyncrasies of the individual and play it that way, whether he was playing cards or anything else, and this is true in life," Hardy said. "You want to figure out the idiosyncrasies of your opponent, whether it's a prizefighter or (whoever) it is."[6]

Hardy learned that Perry prided himself on being the first person to arrive at the bank each

The red-and-white 84 Lumber logo, atop "lollipop"-style signs, became one of the most recognizable in the country.

In the back row of this photo are, from left, Joe Hardy, Norman Hardy, Jack Kunkle, and Bob Hardy. Together with Ed Ryan, the five men were the original partners in 84 Lumber.

day, usually around 8 in the morning, even though the bank did not open until 9.[7] Hardy decided that in order to impress Perry he would have to beat the banker at his own game.

He arrived at the bank at 7 and met Perry at the door when the banker showed up for work.[8] Hardy recalled that Perry was visibly impressed and that throughout their years of dealings, whenever Hardy renewed loans and extended his line of credit, Perry often remarked "By God, you get up early."[9]

After Hardy had secured the loan, it was time to begin building. Hardy calculated what he would need for the business and began making plans. He was joined in his venture by his two brothers, Bob and Norman Hardy, as well as Ed Ryan and an attorney friend named Jack Kunkle.

The five men put their money together to pay for the land and buildings, which, in what may have been a good omen for the company, ended up totaling $84,000.[10] Construction began, and soon the new lumber warehouse in Eighty Four, Pennsylvania, was completed.

Now Joe Hardy had just one problem. After paying for the land and the construction, he had no money left to buy inventory for his new store. However, one of his fellow investors, Jack Kunkle, was ready with a solution.[11] Kunkle had already invested about $14,000 in 84 Lumber,[12] and when Hardy needed more money, Kunkle said[13] he would buy the 84 Lumber building, giving Hardy the cash he needed to buy supplies for the store, and then lease the store to Hardy.[14]

Hardy agreed, under one condition: the sales contract must contain a clause giving Hardy the right to buy the building back in the future, at a price to be fixed at the time of sale.[15] Kunkle agreed, and Hardy began ordering inventory.

Before work could begin at the new building, however, Hardy wanted to finalize one last detail of the arrangement. During his years working at Hardy and Hayes, he had observed many struggles between his father and his Uncle Paul, both of whom had very different visions of how the business should be run.[16]

Hardy decided to avoid the same type of problems with his new business by creating a "buy-and-sell" agreement. This agreement allowed the group to buy out any of the partners at a set price that was recalculated each year, so that if insurmountable differences arose, they could be settled quickly by buying someone out.[17]

Breaking Down Barriers

Once the financing was secured and the business partnership was formalized, the Hardys took over the job of running 84 Lumber. Ryan continued to build houses, and Kunkle's involvement was purely financial. Once again, the three Hardy brothers worked as a team to ensure the business succeeded. Bob Hardy became nominal president of the company, and Norman Hardy ran the office and handled purchasing.

When 84 Lumber was established, only wholesalers could purchase lumber directly from mills, so a second company, Lumber Distributors, was set up to buy from the mills and sell to 84 Lumber. The partners established a third enterprise in Glendale, West Virginia, about an hour from the Pennsylvania border.[18]

There the company converted an old icehouse into a workshop that created pre-hung doors and preassembled Crestline windows to sell at 84 Lumber and other stores.[19] Eventually, however, Hardy decided not to produce materials for other retailers, and the Glendale location became a standard 84 Lumber store.[20]

Once the business details were settled, 84 Lumber began buying its lumber from Canadian mills. During the 19th century, Pennsylvania had been an important logging center.[21] In fact, it is estimated that when Englishman William Penn arrived to settle the area in 1682, almost 90 percent of the commonwealth was forested.[22] Indeed, the name Pennsylvania means "Penn's Woods."

During the late 1800s, however, loggers moved through the state, cutting down vast stands of pine and hemlock,[23] and by the time Hardy established 84 Lumber, Pennsylvania had long since depleted its wood resources. Although small amounts of lumber were obtained locally, most of the company's bulk orders were shipped from western Canada.

Initially, the partners had a difficult time persuading these mills to sell to 84 Lumber. It took all the Hardy brothers' charisma and sales skills to talk the mills into selling to an upstart lumber company, with no reputation to precede it.[24] At the time, most lumber companies were family-owned empires that had been around for years.[25] To the mill owners, 84 Lumber was a risky customer, an unproven challenger to the established system.

Sometimes the company's name was a help, however. Bob Hardy recalled that one mill representative misunderstood when Joe Hardy called and said that he was an owner of the 84 Lumber stores, thinking instead that Hardy owned 84 stores.[26]

By the time Hardy established 84 Lumber, Pennsylvania had depleted most of its wood resources. Most lumberyards in the area obtained lumber from mills in western Canada.

Cash and Carry

Once their new business was up and running, Ryan, Kunkle, and the Hardys did whatever they could to make sure it was successful. The heart of this effort was the cash-and-carry system. Customers had to pay either in cash or with a personal check. If the customer could not "carry" away the goods, 84 Lumber would deliver them for an additional fee. Hardy hired a subcontractor to make the deliveries and charged customers based on the size of the load.[27]

The system worked just as Hardy had hoped it would. Although 84 Lumber took out a few loans throughout the years, the company never accrued any substantial debts because the cash-and-carry system kept the assets flowing. Most of the lumber mills wanted payment on delivery, and 84 Lumber was able to meet that demand.

Although the fledgling lumber company might not have always posted high profits or had much money tucked away, 84 Lumber was not in debt, and unlike the days at Green Hills Lumber, there was always money to pay the bills.

Hand in hand with the cash-and-carry system came 84 Lumber's goal of low prices and high inventory turnover. The Hardy brothers did not want to have too much invested in inventory at any one time. They strove to move products quickly through the store, aiming for a complete turnover of inventory several times a year instead of once or twice, as most other lumberyards did.[28]

In order to achieve this goal, 84 Lumber offered its lowest prices to all of its customers, whether they were individuals working on simple home improvement projects or contractors who built hundreds of homes a year.[29] When contractors complained about the set-up, Bob Hardy explained to them that despite the fact that everyone paid the same price, large contractors were still saving more than individuals because they were buying more.[30]

'Real Good People'

With these basic principles in place, 84 Lumber's owners began to think of other ways to improve their business. One key to the company's success, as with Green Hills Lumber, was the quality and dedication of its employees. Bob Hardy recalled:

We were very, very particular who we hired, and I think probably that's one of the biggest secrets of the thing. We hired real good people. Therefore, we could promote from within. We kept real good people.... Hard-working, down-to-earth people, that [didn't just want] to sit in an office all day, I guess. Hard-working men that wanted a future.[31]

And indeed, several integral players were joining the 84 Lumber team during that time.

Charles "Cap" Moore had just returned from military service and was living at home on his family farm without much to do. A friend told him about Joe Hardy's new business, which at the time was still being built, and Moore sought out Hardy to ask for a job. Moore began as a forklift operator and went on to become manager of the 84 Lumber store the following year. It was the beginning of a long career with the company. After managing stores in Maryland and Ohio, Moore became Northeastern Region manager and then Western Region manager before he retired in 1984.[32]

Charles "Cap" Moore joined 84 Lumber early on and worked for the company until he retired in 1984. He remembered that Joe Hardy was a demanding—but fair—employer.

Another important addition to the 84 Lumber team was Barb Mosi, who joined the company in 1959, when she was just 17 years old and had just graduated from high school. Mosi said that when she began working at the store, there were no businesses along the stretch of road that led to and from the town of Eighty Four, a road that would eventually be filled with 84 Lumber buildings.

She also recalled that in the early days, when the company had relatively few employees, each worker had to pitch in and do a little bit of everything, from stocking inventory to filing paperwork—back when everything was done by hand.

As 2004 approached, Mosi was still working for 84 Lumber and was looking forward to her 45th anniversary with the company,[33] the only place she ever worked. Mosi said she stayed with the company so long because she was always treated fairly and never taken for granted.

"I consider Joe my boss and my friend because he's always been good to me," she said.[34]

Developing Loyalty

Almost immediately, customers began flocking to 84 Lumber from the surrounding area and beyond. The company's task then became finding ways to develop customer loyalty.

Despite his strict adherence to cash-and-carry policies, Hardy understood that some clients would not be able to pay their entire bill at one time, so the company introduced a prepayment plan.

Once again, it was necessary to spend some time convincing contractors, who were used to buying on credit, that paying in advance made sense. In order to sweeten the deal, 84 Lumber introduced a 90-day price protection plan, which guaranteed contractors a set price during that period.

A common problem for building contractors was that the price of lumber fluctuated on a daily basis.[35] Most contractors quoted clients a price for a homebuilding project before the project began,[36] but if the price of lumber rose substantially during the course of the project, the contractor could end up with a smaller profit than anticipated.[37]

84 Lumber created a plan whereby customers who prepaid "locked in" the price of the lumber they were buying for the next 90 days.[38] By offering price protection, Hardy gave his clients a chance to safe-

Barb Mosi joined 84 Lumber, the only place she has ever worked, in 1959. In her current position of assistant treasurer, she manages the company's 401(k) and profit-sharing programs, and handles other accounting work.

guard their profits, while gaining for himself the security of prepaid orders.

In addition, Cap Moore recalled that as committed as Joe Hardy was to the principle of cash and carry, store managers sometimes bent the rules for loyal customers without the boss's knowledge. Moore said:

Occasionally, the manager took it on himself to give somebody a little credit until they got their house... to keep him coming. You didn't want to tell him, "Well, no, I'm not going to give you that unless I see the cash," because after a while, I think, you knew he was good for it.[39]

Eventually, however, Hardy instituted a system of moving store managers frequently from location to location, in part to prevent precisely this type of favoritism toward clients.[40]

ORIGIN OF EIGHTY FOUR'S NAME STILL A MYSTERY

JOE HARDY WAS FOND OF TELLING PEOple that he named his company after the town of Eighty Four, Pennsylvania, because he thought the name had a magic ring to it.[1]

But if the town name came first, the question remains, why was the town called Eighty Four? Eighty Four, Pennsylvania, is one of a handful of towns with numbers for names, along with Eighty Eight in Kentucky, and One-Hundred-and-One Ranch in Missouri. The definitive reason for christening the town Eighty Four has been lost to history, but several theories remain, some of them more plausible than others.

The most widely accepted theory holds that the town was named to honor President Grover Cleveland's election in 1884. Eighty Four is located on the Baltimore and Ohio railroad line, and one of its earliest buildings was a post office owned by William J. Smith.[2]

According to one source, Smith owned a mill and later a store located near the railroad.[3] When he opened the post office and became the local postmaster, he applied to have the office named "Smithville."[4] However, he was informed that there was already a post office of that name in Pennsylvania.[5]

While visiting the Burgettstown Fair in 1885, he discussed the naming problem with a Mr. Lewis Armstrong, who suggested giving the new post office a numeric name.[6] Smith decided on Eighty Four in honor of President Cleveland's election the previous year, and as the town grew the name stuck.[7]

Some of the other theories regarding the name are that the town is located 80 degrees and 4 minutes west longitude, or that George Washington located a saloon at 84 degrees west of the general store during a 1740 surveying trip.[8]

Some say that the village is located on the 84th tract of land carved out by the Northwest Ordinance, or that the town was mail drop number 84 on the Railway Mail Service.[9] One theory that can be decisively disproved is the rumor that the town got its name because Joe Hardy played for the Green Bay Packers football team and wore jersey number 84.[10]

Whatever the reason for the name, the connection has proved useful to both 84 Lumber and Eighty Four, Pennsylvania. In the early days of the 84 Lumber company, the name was a sort of marketing tool, reminding customers exactly where the store was located.[11] In return, 84 Lumber has garnered widespread attention for the small town in southwestern Pennsylvania.

To this day, Eighty Four remains a small rural town, comprised mostly of farms and a few stores. The one notable exception to this, of course, is 84 Lumber, whose bright red "lollipop" style signs have made the name of the little town famous across the United States.[12]

84 Lumber management also went to great lengths to provide customer convenience. The company had a relatively small number of employees, and as the number of customers increased, these associates worked long and hard to make sure that all clients were satisfied.

84 Lumber's salespeople were knowledgeable about do-it-yourself home improvements and often helped customers plan their renovation projects.[41] Joe Hardy also set an example for all his workers by starting his days early, sometimes at 4 A.M., and staying as late as necessary to make sure that things were done properly.

In addition, a system was developed whereby a crew of workers assembled customer orders at night for morning pickup, bundling together all the lumber, doors, and other materials needed for a particular order.[42]

This process helped increase turnover, which was essential to making the cash-and-carry system work, and was also convenient for customers who wanted to begin working on their projects first thing in the morning. However, the hectic schedule took its toll on the workers.

Cap Moore recalled, "I remember back when we started. I was there pretty much by myself trying to service customers and unload trucks and unload boxcars of lumber, but I would work till 11 or 12 [at night], and then I would get up, and I would get back here at 4 in the morning."[43]

Although Hardy was a demanding employer, his workers recalled that he was always fair. When Moore eventually told Hardy that he would have to quit working for 84 Lumber because he was unable to meet the rigorous demands of the company, Hardy immediately gave Moore a raise and hired more workers to assist him.[44]

A final strategy for success was to stick to the basics. Initially, 84 Lumber provided lumber and not much else. Lumber arrived at the yard already cut and was usually sold in exactly the same condition as it arrived on the train cars from the mills.[45] Some items, such as trim, were purchased from local producers, and the store also carried a few hardware items, such as nails and hinges.[46]

But for the most part, the Hardys stuck to what they knew best and made sure that they had experienced sales staff who knew about the inventory and how to use it.

Hardys Take Control

As 84 Lumber continued to grow, Hardy began to reevaluate his arrangement with his business partners. He was happy working with his brothers and Ed Ryan but had doubts about the fifth partner, Jack Kunkle.

After being in business a few years, Hardy could tell that 84 Lumber was going to be a tremendous success, and he worried that Kunkle would want to take the company public, making 84 Lumber subject to the demands of stockholders instead of those of Hardy himself.[47]

Accordingly, he determined to find a way to get Kunkle to sell his share of the business as specified in the buy-and-sell agreement. Finally, Hardy hit upon a plan and went to Ed Ryan for help.

I said to my friend, Ed, "Ed, I can't get this guy out." He said, "OK, Joe, I'll tell you what I'll do. I'll sell my stock to you, and that will embarrass him, and therefore he'll sell it to you." So we did buy Ed out for, at that time, probably an equivalent thing for maybe $87,000.

So Ed went to Jack and said, "Well, gee, I know this Joe. I really think he really wants to get everybody out of here and is sort of dippy about it. So gee, Jack, I agreed to sell mine with the buy-and-sell, which is certainly, Jack, a very reasonable appreciation of what your investment was."

So Jack finally agreed to sell at something much even greater though than I had paid. ... He still mutters about it because his would have been worth at least a couple hundred million at least.[48]

With both Ryan and Kunkle having sold their shares, 84 Lumber was owned completely by Joe, Bob, and Norman Hardy, and the company was ready to enter a new phase of expansion and development.

Joe Hardy recognized the importance of attending his stores' grand opening events, which were often attended by local politicians and members of the press. In 50 years, he had not missed one opening, even flying around the country to attend 20 of them in a day and a half in 2002.

CHAPTER FIVE

GROWING AND CHANGING

One of the reasons Dad says he's very successful is because he had a number of failures, and so he learns from every failure. I think it is his vision, sometimes flawed vision, [that makes him succeed]. ... He keeps trying.

—Robin Freed, Joe Hardy's daughter

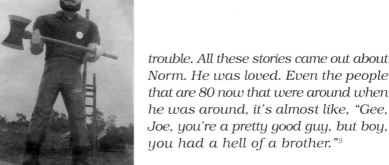

WHILE JOE HARDY'S BUSI-ness was evolving and expanding, several important events occurred in his personal life as well. During the 1960s, two major changes came about that would affect both Hardy and 84 Lumber.

The first was the death of Hardy's brother Norman in a plane crash in November 1962.[1] Several months prior to the tragedy, Joe Hardy had taken an interest in flying, and Norman soon learned to fly a single-engine Mooney aircraft.[2] After receiving his flying license, Norman Hardy took his young son to Pennsylvania's Washington Airport for a practice flight.[3] Their plane encountered a snow squall and crashed, killing them both.[4]

His brother's death made a huge impact on Joe Hardy, who realized that up until that point, he had considered himself somehow invincible. For the first time, he began seriously thinking about succession plans for 84 Lumber. Joe Hardy recalled that in the wake of the accident, many friends and associates revealed that Norman had helped them financially and otherwise in times of need but had never claimed any credit. Inspired by his brother's example, Hardy would go on to help many others in difficult circumstances. Hardy said of his brother:

When [Norman] was killed, there were different [stories] that [surfaced about how] he helped pay for this person that was getting this trouble and that

trouble. All these stories came out about Norm. He was loved. Even the people that are 80 now that were around when he was around, it's almost like, "Gee, Joe, you're a pretty good guy, but boy, you had a hell of a brother."[5]

Norman Hardy was also fondly remembered by employees as one of the only people who could match Joe Hardy for vitality and determination. Cap Moore, recalling Norman's amazing sales abilities, said, "He was a fireball, ... a sweet talker! ... He was energetic and an excellent salesman. I mean the guy, he could sell anything."[6]

During those years, there was joy as well as sadness for the Hardy family. The couple were in their early 40s when they learned that they would soon have another child. During her pregnancy, Dottie grew so large that the Hardys' friends thought she was having twins and joked that they'd be named "Cash" and "Carry."[7] But on December 7, 1965, the Hardys welcomed a single child—Maggie—to the family.

The couple's long-time friend Betty Gottschalk recalled that, although the Hardys had assumed their family was complete, Maggie turned out to be "the biggest blessing they ever had."[8]

A giant fiberglass statue of Paul Bunyan presided over 84 Lumber grand openings as the company expanded across the country.

Maggie Hardy, seen here with her father, Joe, began training for an executive position at 84 Lumber from a young age, when she began accompanying her dad to the lumberyard.

Like Father, Like Daughter

From the beginning, Joe and Maggie seemed to have a special bond. From the time that Maggie was just seven years old, Hardy started taking her to the lumberyard to learn about how his business worked, and she soon began attending board meetings and 84 Lumber grand openings.[9]

Because Maggie's oldest brother, Joe Jr., was nearly 20 years her senior, Maggie was almost the same age as her nephew, Joe Jr.'s son, Alex Hardy. As children, Maggie and Alex accompanied Joe Hardy on trips around the country in a motorhome, searching for new 84 Lumber sites.[10]

Alex Hardy recalled his grandfather drove like a madman, tearing down highways and back country roads alike,[11] but despite his hurry to get where he was going, Joe Hardy refused to travel by plane.[12]

On more than one occasion, this wild driving style landed Hardy in hot water—and once it even landed him in jail. He recalled one grand opening, when he had brought his mother along. They were riding in a Mustang through a small town in Ohio when a police officer pulled them over about 2 A.M. The officer thought he smelled beer, and since the town's magistrate wasn't scheduled to come on duty until 9, the officer took the mother and son to jail.

As they waited in adjoining cells, Hardy said his mother told him it was his fault they were in jail because he had chosen to drive the Mustang.

"She said, 'You know, you don't use your head. Why did you bring that little Muskrat up?' She called it a Muskrat. 'That's why they caught you.'"[13]

Alex Hardy remembered Maggie as aggressive and outgoing, with a wild streak that livened up the long road trips.[14]

All of the time Joe Hardy's daughter spent on these site-finding expeditions, as well as weekends accompanying her father to work, would prove to be excellent training for the little girl who would grow up to become president of 84 Lumber. As long-time employee Bink Conover put it, "That was her college education, just following Dad around."[15]

Later, Maggie Hardy Magerko would recall that work and play were never separate pursuits—84 Lumber was simply a way of life. She remembered, however, that receiving her first paycheck—when she was still in elementary school—was a thrill.

"I probably never even cashed it because I can remember showing my Mom how proud I was getting a little paycheck," Hardy Magerko said.[16]

Sound Investments

Throughout the 1960s, 84 Lumber continued to expand. Joe Hardy visited surrounding areas and eventually other states in search of the perfect sites on which to build new stores. With many of

Above: Jeanene Tomshay began as a clerical worker in the advertising department. During her 30 years with 84 Lumber, she became the first woman in management and developed the company's training program.

Below: Dan Hixenbaugh, left, shown here with George and Edna Handyside, joined 84 Lumber in 1964 and went on to become the company's director of advertising and public relations.

these locations, Hardy adopted a similar buy-and-lease-back arrangement that had worked so successfully with Jack Kunkle.[17]

In each new market Hardy did some research and found an investor willing to buy a store building and lease it back to him.[18] It was a sound investment for the buyer and gave Hardy the cash flow he needed to continue expanding his business. But Hardy was always adamant that he be able to buy the buildings back at a pre-set price. This strategy served him well, and the company's real estate holdings came to represent millions of dollars.

In one instance, an investor was reluctant to buy a building knowing that he might eventually be required to sell it back.[19] The building was worth about $6,000 at the time, and Hardy told the prospective buyer to name the highest number he could think of as the buyback price.[20] A selling price of $200,000 was agreed upon.[21] By the time the agree-

ment matured and Hardy was ready to buy, however, he recalled that the building was worth $400,000![22]

Jack Knight, who later worked as general counsel for 84 Lumber, noted that this practice, as well as many others, always worked to give Hardy the upper hand.

"The banks would come to us begging to loan us money instead of the other way around," Knight said. "I mean our interest rate, when we did borrow, was unbelievably low. It was below the prime rate."[23]

While new lumberyards were being established, the 84 Lumber family was also expanding. Once again, employees were joining the 84 Lumber team who would make the company their life's work and help Joe Hardy bring his vision to life.

Jeanene Tomshay began working at 84 Lumber two weeks after graduating from Saint Elizabeth High School, located in Pittsburgh's Pleasant Hills suburb, in 1964.[24] As teenagers, her brothers had helped unload boxcars at Green Hills Lumber, so she had heard of Joe Hardy before.[25]

Now she began as a clerical worker in the advertising department.[26] Tomshay, who remembered a time in which she was the only woman to attend management meetings, would eventually design an 84 Lumber training program, become head of the advertising department, and spend a total of 30 years with 84 Lumber.[27]

The same year, Dan Hixenbaugh, a long-time friend of Hardy's, began working at 84 Lumber. Hixenbaugh recalled a sense of foreboding when, after he accepted the position, the details of the job were discussed.

"My alarm bells [started ringing] when [Hardy] said, 'You can start on Sunday. And be there about 6 in the morning because we'll be taking inventory,' which was an all-day job. With that, I thought, 'Oh, boy, what am I getting into here?' "[28]

Hixenbaugh proved equal to the task, however, and went on to become 84 Lumber's director of advertising and public relations.

Cecil Gravely came in to interview at an 84 Lumber store in St. Albans, West Virginia, one Thursday in 1967, and by the following Tuesday found himself being shipped off to Illinois to begin work as a manager trainee.[29] As luck would have it, the Illinois store was having its grand opening, and Joe Hardy arrived at the store the very next day.[30]

The lumberyard was packed with customers who were having trouble finding parking spaces, and Hardy made a first impression on the new employee that Gravely never forgot.

Somebody said something to Joe about how are we going to park all these cars, and Joe said, "I'll show you how we're going to park all these cars. Give me that pair of gloves." This guy had an orange pair of gloves. Joe throws them on. Puts his cigar in his mouth. Goes out to the main gate. Starts flipping his hands, right and left, and here and there. So Joe went out and parked the cars.[31]

Gravely eventually returned to St. Albans and became manager of that 84 Lumber location. As of

2003, he had been at the St. Albans store for 30 years, the longest time that anyone at 84 Lumber has been manager of the same store.[32]

Gail Baughman was born and grew up on a farm in Ohio.[33] After finishing college, he found himself looking for a job and applied at an 84 Lumber store in Vanport, Pennsylvania,[34] a one-hour commute from his home.[35] Baughman recalled that when he showed up for his first day of work he still had long hair from his college days.[36] His 84 Lumber manager took one look at him and told him to get a haircut and a decent pair of work shoes before returning the next day.[37]

Following this rocky start, however, Baughman went on to become a stellar employee. From a starting salary of $84 a week, he quickly worked his way up to be a store co-manager,[38] and soon afterward he was promoted to manager of the Albany, New York, store.

Left: Cecil Gravely had been manager of the St. Albans, West Virginia, store for 30 years, the longest time that anyone at 84 Lumber had been manager of the same store.

Below: Gail Baughman, right—who served as store manager in Eighty Four, Pennsylvania, for 25 years—received the Manager of the Year award in 1990.

He was 84 Lumber's youngest manager and recalled that because he was not yet 21 years old, he was not even eligible for the company's 401(k) retirement plan.[39] Baughman would go on to be store manager in Eighty Four, Pennsylvania, for 25 years.[40]

Baughman recalled that while this was an advantageous position because workers at the Eighty Four location always had the first opportunity to try out new products and ideas, it was also a demanding one because he was constantly under Hardy's watchful eye.[41]

No Frills

While plenty of money was being invested in expansion, Joe Hardy established, from the beginning, a no-frills approach at 84 Lumber that would allow him to keep his costs low and thereby offer lower prices to his customers.

All 84 Lumber buildings were so simply constructed that they were essentially large lumber sheds with racks to hold supplies. Hardy also saved money by refusing to install heating or air conditioning units in any of his lumber stores.

Bink Conover recalled that Hardy used to tell him, "People ought to be moving fast enough that they don't have time to get cold."[42]

Some managers in chillier locales, however, lacked Hardy's enthusiasm for thrift. Gail Baughman recalled that when he managed the store in Albany, New York, he kept a small space heater hidden under the counter during the coldest winter months.[43] One time, he said, Joe Hardy Jr. visited the store unexpectedly and found Baughman and his workers all huddled around the small heater.[44] Joe Jr. gave a good-natured wink, and the space heater remained a secret from his father.[45]

At times, the cold conditions inside the store were the least of Baughman's problems. One winter, an especially heavy snowstorm caused the store's roof to cave in. He recalled:

When 84 Lumber added some home improvement products to its inventory, the stores became more comfortable than the early lumberyards. Still, all stores were constructed as simply as possible in order to keep prices low.

So we have this hole now in the roof that's probably 40 to 50 feet long and half the building. So I called up the office. It's on a Saturday morning. Told them who I was. … [A man came] up on Monday with his crew. We polyethylened in the interior of the store where this hole was, and we opened it back up for business on Tuesday. We had no heat and no bathrooms till May. I'm not kidding you. It was something. We just told people we were under construction for remodeling.[46]

Employees at 84 Lumber headquarters also made do with less than luxurious accommodations. Rose Pournaras, who worked in the Sales Accounting Department, remembered, "We didn't have any carpeting. It was just plank floors. There were gaps in between. So if you wore any kind of a shoe with a heel, your shoe would go down between the cracks. If you would drop money or jewelry or anything, it would go down in the cracks, and then they'd have to pry the boards up to get the stuff out."[47]

Her husband, Chris, a computer programmer who was approaching his 26th year at the company, recalled keeping his personal belongings in a wooden slot next to his desk. In the cramped quarters, his work was often interrupted by people opening the office door and banging the back of his chair.

"Even the auditors when they'd come in, they'd ask if they could wear old clothes because we had old wood tables back then, and they'd get their nylons stuck on it," he said.[48]

Another classic example of Joe Hardy's cost-conscious approach to business was his response to a flowerbed that needed attention outside a company building.

Dan Wallach, who later worked as Chief Financial Officer of 84 Lumber, remembered, "Instead of paying someone to weed it, all the employees would go out for like 10 minutes, and we'd all weed the garden to save 100 bucks or whatever it would have cost for someone to take care of it."

Not only did this strategy save the company money, but it also instilled in employees a valuable business lesson. "It taught you that everything was cheap," Wallach said. "Not only was price negotiable, but there were other ways to get things done that didn't cost anything."[49]

That situation, as well as the company's response to Baughman's winter woes, were typical of the can-do attitude that permeated 84 Lumber. That same spirit meant that Hardy was always looking for ways to expand and improve his business.

84 Junction

During its first few years in business, 84 Lumber remained committed to the principle of keeping its inventory uncomplicated, selling only lumber and a few other basic items. Eventually, however, Hardy began to wonder whether it might be wise to expand the stores' offerings, so he devised an experiment to determine what types of merchandise should be introduced into 84 Lumber's inventory.[50]

To lead the project, Hardy tapped Jeanene Tomshay, who had only been working at the company for a few months when she was called into Hardy's office to discuss her new assignment. Tomshay, who had feared she was about to lose her job, was instead promoted to office manager of what Hardy called Department X,[51] a venture that would later become an 84 Junction store.[52]

84 Junction was so named because its original building was located at the intersection of Pennsylvania state routes 519 and 136, in the heart of Eighty Four, Pennsylvania.[53] The store was stocked with every item imaginable as Hardy sought to find out what types of goods his customers were interested in.

84 Junction sold some home improvement items, such as kitchen and bath fixtures and paint.[54] But the store also carried appliances, work clothing, and cosmetics.[55] An entire section of toys was added,[56] and a tack shop, with saddles and the like for local farmers, was situated in another area of the store.[57] Because of 84 Junction's rural location, the store took the place of an old-fashioned general store or a modern-day Wal-Mart, providing everything customers needed in one location when there were few other stores nearby.

Initially the venture was successful, and the company formulated a plan to expand 84 Junction. Hardy brought in new workers to assist Tomshay, including Bob MacKinney, an employee who had joined 84 Lumber as a seasonal Christmas worker at 84 Junction.[58] After the holiday season, Hardy offered MacKinney a chance to work at a lumberyard in Indiana, but MacKinney wanted to stay near Eighty Four.[59] He was given a permanent position at 84 Junction, and when new stores were proposed, he helped Tomshay with the expansion plans.[60]

New 84 Junction stores were built next to existing 84 lumberyards in various locations,[61] and the name of the enterprise was changed from 84 Junction to 84 Home Center.[62] Eventually, more than 20 84 Home Centers were providing customers with just about everything they needed for their home projects and their daily lives.[63]

However, after a while it became clear that the stores were not generating enough profit to justify maintaining them as separate entities, and Tomshay integrated the most popular products from the 84 Home Centers into the inventory at the regular 84 Lumber stores.[64]

Throughout the years, the best-selling Home Center items had been kitchen and bath supplies,[65] which had even helped to supplement lumberyard

Inset: 84 Lumber buildings were essentially large lumber sheds without heating or air conditioning.

Below: 84 Home Centers offered various types of merchandise, from home improvement items to appliances, clothing, cosmetics, and toys.

income during winter months, when purchases of building supplies decreased.[66]

These items became part of the inventory at 84 Lumber, but sales of toys and personal items ceased. After the Home Centers closed, Tomshay became a specialties buyer for all of the 84 lumberyards and was responsible for choosing and ordering all kitchen, bathroom, and plumbing items, as well as paint.[67] She recalled that the job was challenging but that Joe Hardy's confidence in her gave her the drive to do her best. Tomshay said:

> *Joe gave a person their head. In other words, if you were good enough to have responsibility, you were good enough to make your own decisions. ... The greatest gift that Joe has given to me is a lifetime of opportunity and challenges and the empowering belief that I could do it. In other words, he believed in me. So I, in turn, figured, my goodness, I can do this. Joe believes in me.[68]*

Even though the venture was not ultimately successful on its own, employees such as Tomshay, as well as Hardy himself, learned some important business lessons from the 84 Junction project.

Robin Freed, Hardy's daughter, spent three summers while in high school working at 84 Junction,[69] her first job with the company.[70] In reflecting on her father's career in the lumber industry and experiments like 84 Junction, she remarked:

> *One of the reasons Dad says he's very successful is because he had a number of failures, and so he learns from every failure. ... I think it is his vision. Vision sometimes is flawed. ... There's another place I worked for [with] 84. It was called Lifestyle 84. That didn't work either. That was in Pittsburgh, and it was supposed to be kind of like Macy's Cellar, and that only lasted three years also. ... But I think it is his vision, sometimes flawed vision, [that makes him succeed]. ... He keeps trying.[71]*

Getting the Word Out

While Hardy was busy amassing a collection of talented employees and experimenting with new business ideas, he never forgot that the key to success in any business is to gain and retain customers. As 84 Lumber expanded into new markets, its advertising department worked overtime to find ways to reach new customers—both individuals and contractors.

Bink Conover was in charge of writing copy for newspaper ads and then placing the advertisements, which often proved to be a challenging task. Because many of the local lumberyards were family-owned enterprises that had been around for years, some newspapers were reluctant to run ads for an upstart company like 84 Lumber that challenged the security and prosperity of these established businesses.[72]

Fortunately, Hardy augmented traditional newspaper ads with more innovative types of marketing including radio ads.[73] In addition, a local

Left: Bob MacKinney began working for the company as a seasonal worker at 84 Junction. He went on to become manager of the 84 Lumber store in Waynesburg, Pennsylvania.

Opposite: Flags fly to welcome visitors to an 84 Lumber grand opening. Word-of-mouth advertising generated by the events helped the company draw crowds and build up its customer mailing lists.

SIGNS POINT THE WAY TO 84 LUMBER

WITHOUT A DOUBT, 84 LUMBER'S most well-known advertising tool was its distinctive 84 Lumber directional sign. Employees tacked these small, rectangular metal signs—measuring about one-and-a-half by two-and-a-half feet—to trees, fences, and anything else that would serve as a roadside signpost.[1]

The signs bore the red-and-white 84 Lumber logo, along with an arrow pointing in the direction of the nearest 84 Lumber store. In the weeks before a store grand opening, 84 Lumber employees would pepper all the roads around the store with directional signs to help drum up excitement about the new business.

The signs were a practical way of helping customers who were actually trying to find an 84 Lumber store and a clever tactic to pique the interest of casual passersby who had never heard of the company. They generated a great deal of attention to the 84 Lumber name, but the attention given was not always of the type that Joe Hardy wanted.

Some municipalities did not appreciate the unsolicited and unapproved advertising for 84 Lumber.[2] Environmental groups complained that the signs were an eyesore. Some communities ordered 84 Lumber to remove the signs and even fined the company for posting them without permission.[3]

However, it would have been difficult to find a community whose determination to remove the signs matched Hardy's determination to put them up. He offered employees cash bonuses for each sign posted.[4] After a while, annual directional sign competitions were held to see which employee could post the most signs,[5] and some employees put up hundreds and even thousands of signs.[6]

Eventually—especially in western Pennsylvania—84 Lumber directional signs could be seen even in areas where there was no 84 Lumber store for many miles,[7] and the 84 Lumber logo became one of the most recognizable in the country.[8]

"They're everywhere in Pennsylvania," said Judy Donohue, who worked as director of corporate communications and public relations for 84 Lumber. "You don't even know where it points, but just an arrow pointing to 84 Lumber because you know there's going to be one somewhere."[9]

television station offered commercial spots at low prices, and Hardy took advantage of these to bring in customers from far beyond Eighty Four, Pennsylvania, and even from out of state.[74]

Mailings were another major aspect of the effort. The company sent out broadsides that advertised 84 Lumber's low prices, taking special care to personally address each piece, a process that involved stenciling each customer's name onto a card by hand and imprinting the names using a special machine.[75]

Finally, signs were placed along the roadsides near each new 84 Lumber store that pointed in the direction of the lumberyard. These signs soon

became well known in Eighty Four, Pennsylvania, and eventually throughout the country.

However, more spectacular by far than any of 84 Lumber's other advertising methods were its grand opening celebrations. These events, conducted as each new lumberyard opened for business, drew people from throughout the community for days of fun and entertainment.

There were competitions, performers, food, and music to draw crowds and publicize the presence of the new lumberyard. The company sent out flyers weeks in advance to let local residents know about the upcoming event. 84 Lumber employees and the company's suppliers, who also attended the grand openings, posted hundreds of 84 Lumber directional signs in the days leading up to the event.[76]

In the early days of 84 Lumber, Hardy and Dan Hixenbaugh drove to many of the openings in an old Volkswagen bus with an aluminum boat, one of the prizes to be awarded at the event, strapped to the roof. Hixenbaugh remembered reading aloud to Hardy to keep him awake during the long drives.[77]

Above: Associates wait to greet local residents at an 84 Lumber grand opening. The events were a great way for the company to make a name for itself in a new community.

Right: Grand openings were a combination of circus, neighborhood barbeque, home repair class, and Olympic competition. Families often attended and spent the day there together.

On the day of the grand opening, anyone driving past the new 84 Lumber would be greeted by Hardy's children and grandchildren, as well as the children of other 84 Lumber employees, wearing clown costumes, waving to drivers, and doing their part to help draw passersby to the celebration.[78] In some locations, a hot-air balloon with the 84 Lumber logo floated above the store to mark the location of the festivities.[79]

Local churches and charitable organizations were invited to staff concession stands.[80] 84 Lumber provided the food, and the charities were allowed to keep the profits.[81] In the early days, coffee and hotdogs were sold for a nickel.[82]

In order to advertise 84 Lumber's products, grand openings usually played host to a number of demonstrations. Companies that supplied products to 84 lumberyards would send representatives to demonstrate those products.[83]

According to Bill Fulton, who worked as operations manager, these vendors "were very instrumental

Opposite: An inflatable Paul Bunyan eventually took the place of the original fiberglass statue.

Right: All qualifiers in the Paul Bunyan games were awarded $5, finalists in each event won $25, and the overall winner, who earned the title 'Mr. Paul Bunyan,' received a grand prize of $84.

Below: Crosscut sawing was another contest featured in the popular Paul Bunyan games. Participants got the chance to compete in the events while they honed their home improvement skills.

in attending grand openings and being a part of the whole scheme of things." Through the demonstration workshops, suppliers got to advertise their products and spectators learned some useful home improvement skills.[84]

Unusual Attractions

The openings were also the occasion for a series of events known as the Paul Bunyan games, contests in such traditional lumberjack skills as log-rolling, crosscut sawing, nail driving, fishing-line casting, and tobacco spitting.[85] Hixenbaugh used a trailer to haul a giant fiberglass statue of Paul Bunyan, which presided over the contests and celebrations at each grand opening.[86]

The competitions usually lasted for several days, and on Saturdays the finalists in each event competed for the title of Mr. Paul Bunyan.[87] All qualifiers were awarded $5, finalists in each event won $25, and Mr. Paul Bunyan collected a grand prize of $84.

The grand opening celebrations included other attractions, as well, the most popular of which was Victor, the Wrestling Bear. The five-foot black bear was advertised as part of the festivities, and Hixenbaugh recalled that people often arrived days in advance of the grand opening to sign up for a chance to wrestle the bear.[88] Participants received a T-shirt with a picture of Victor and the saying, "I wrestled Victor, the Wrestling Bear, at 84 Lumber Company."[89]

Several other entertainers were remembered fondly by employees many years later. These included Benny "Boom Boom" Koske, the Human Bomb, who would climb into a small wooden box that was subsequently blown up.[90] After an 84 Lumber opening, many local newspapers featured photos of Koske, stunned and smoking but unharmed as he emerged from the remains of the box.

Entertainer Dixie Blandy sat on a small table atop a flagpole for the duration of the grand opening,[91]

84 Lumber grand openings featured popular attractions such as Victor, the Wrestling Bear, who drew local residents days in advance of the events. Benny "Boom Boom" Koske would climb into a small wooden box, which would then be blown up. *(Photo courtesy of The Dominion Post, Morgantown, WV)*

and the Great Wallendas wowed audiences with their acrobatic stunts.[92]

Naturally, such spectacles drew huge crowds from surrounding areas. In the rural areas where 84 Lumber built its lumberyards, the grand openings were a combination of circus, neighborhood barbeque, home repair class, and Olympic competition. Families attended and spent the day at the opening together. The grand openings became so popular with some participants that they would attend every opening in their area.[93]

Word-of-mouth advertising generated by grand openings was extremely helpful to the young company, which took advantage of every opportunity to build its substantial customer mailing list. Local residents were left with a favorable impression of the new business, and 84 Lumber did a spectacular job of imprinting its location in the minds of potential customers.

Hardy recognized the importance of these grand opening events, which were often attended by local politicians and members of the press. Hardy knew that it was crucial to mingle with these important allies, as well as with his future customers, and he made a point of attending each and every grand opening. Hardy said that in the 50-year history of 84 Lumber, he had never missed an opening.[94]

"Joe was right in the mix," said Mike Figgins, regional vice president for 84 Lumber's Central Region. Of the day Figgins first met Hardy, he said, "I remember Joe greeting and talking to the customers as they parked to come into the store."[95]

In 2002, Hardy purchased several buildings at an auction that became new 84 Lumber stores, and the company planned 20 grand openings in one day. Hardy, along with his daughter Maggie, flew

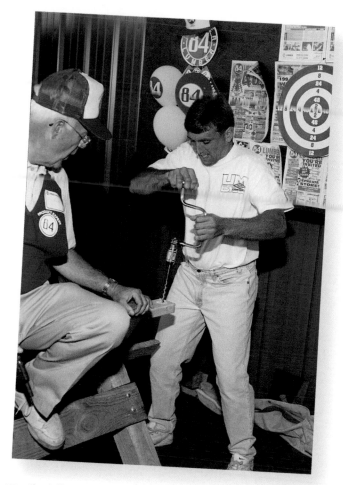

The Paul Bunyan games featured contests in such traditional lumberjack skills as logrolling, as well as nail driving, fishing-line casting, and tobacco spitting.

around the country in his private jet and attended all 20 grand openings in a day and a half, taking advantage of changing time zones.[96]

A 1979 Roman Orgy party at Joe Hardy's home rewarded employees for their long-term service to the company. The event featured authentic Italian food and a toga contest with the grand prize of a bus trip to Rome, New York.

CHAPTER SIX

MOVING AT A HECTIC PACE

You just have to make it happen. … And you don't tell Joe, "I can't do it."

—Cecil Gravely, 84 Lumber manager

AS 84 LUMBER GREW, JOE HARDY was constantly looking for new areas in which he could expand the business. This often created a hectic schedule for his managers. One lesson that any 84 Lumber employee learned early in his or her career with the company was never to tell Joe Hardy that something could not be done.

Bud Weber, an employee who joined 84 Lumber in 1970, recalled, "Joe, even in the early years, was just very, very enthusiastic. He was determined, and he had that little phrase that 'nothing is impossible,' and that's how we operated."[1]

For Hardy, building 84 Lumber was not just a job, it was a way of life. He never held back in his efforts to expand and strengthen his business. Business meetings at 6 A.M. on a Saturday were not uncommon nor were long road trips spent searching for new business opportunities. And Hardy expected his employees to share his boundless enthusiasm for the company.

84 Lumber store managers often led semi-nomadic lives as the company expanded into new markets. For a time, managers were required to move every two to three years.[2] This policy was developed in part to "clean house" and prevent managers from feeling obligated to extend credit to long-time customers.[3]

But it was also because of Joe Hardy's strong commitment to promoting from within the company.

Employees who joined as associates could quickly climb the ladder to become assistant managers, co-managers and eventually regional managers, but they had to be willing to move to whichever store had a job opening.

Promotions were often announced with just a few days' notice. Phil Drake, who later became Hardy's son–in–law when he married Joe's daughter Kathy, remembered joining the company after an interview in Louisville, Kentucky. By the following Monday, Drake had quit school and his part–time job, and had moved to Lexington, Kentucky, to start work. About a year later, he had an opportunity to move to a job at corporate headquarters. He recalled:

I got a call, and it was George Handyside, and he wanted to know if I'd be interested in a job in the corporate office, and I said, "Well, yeah." … He said, "Well, can you be here in three days?" And I said, "Not really, no. I've got to pack, and I've got a lift here, and its's going to take me a while to

---

An 84 Lumber associate displays a prize catch during a Globetrotters reward trip to Kokomo Beach. The trips were just one part of an incentive program developed during the 1970s to help motivate employees to meet their goals.

get everything moved to Pittsburgh." He said, "OK, I'll give you three-and-a-half days."[4]

Moving quickly up the ladder was typical at 84 Lumber, according to Bill Myrick, who had trouble identifying a 2x6 piece of lumber when he started with the company and went on to become chief operating officer. He said that rotating through several different jobs was good training for future company executives:

You experience it from the bottom. ... You can relate to people in each and every job... you're trying to supervise. When you're a co-manager, you can talk to a trainee about his job, because you know what? You were a trainee. When you're a manager, you can talk to a trainee... and if you become an area manager, you can talk to a manager about running the floor because you did his job.[5]

Many managers were eager to move on to stores in bigger markets, and when 84 Lumber was separated into regional divisions, there was fierce but good-natured competition among regional managers to increase sales.[6]

Last-minute moves and sales contests were not the only ways in which employees were required to think on their feet. A combination of planning and flexibility was one of the foundations upon which Hardy built his empire, and he expected his employees to follow suit.

Employees recalled that Hardy required them to have a written agenda at all times, showing predicted deadlines and timelines for all current projects.[7] Furthermore, anyone who showed up at a meeting with Hardy without a pen and paper in hand soon found himself being sent back out to obtain these supplies from one of the secretaries.[8]

"You would never walk into his office without a yellow tablet. That would be the end," said Dan Wallach, Chief Financial Officer. "It would show that

Joe and Maggie Hardy pose for a fun family photo with Maggie's sitter, "Punchy." Joe Hardy's children remembered their father as being lots of fun, but he never neglected an opportunity to teach them lessons about business, as well as life.

you didn't care what he had to say."[9]

But at the same time, Hardy was legendary for his spur-of-the-moment trips. When inspiration struck he never hesitated to take action, whether it be a Sunday, holiday or in the middle of the night, and his managers often found themselves swept along with Hardy's exuberant explorations.

The Fine Art of Site Selection

Nowhere was this more true than with site-finding expeditions. Hardy liked to choose all future 84 Lumber sites personally and spent much of his time traveling around the country in search of promising sites. Among the factors that influenced site decisions was the amount of land made available for purchase. Initially, sites required only three to four acres of land, but as the business grew, inventory expanded to include large items such as house-building kits, until new sites required about 10 acres.[10]

Also in the early years, all 84 lumberyards were built near railroad tracks.[11] This cut down on shipping costs by eliminating the need for delivery trucks,[12] and it also meant that most stores would be located in rural locations.[13] At the same time, it was important to choose a site with enough visibility to attract customers.[14]

In addition, there were zoning restrictions to be considered, which became more important as the years progressed. Because 84 Lumber stores consisted of open lumberyards, some communities did not find them attractive, and zoning was often a struggle.[15]

When choosing a new store site, Hardy sometimes purchased land or buildings from other companies, but more often he sought out unimproved land that he felt would be a good location for an 84 Lumber. He preferred to buy directly from landowners rather than from real estate agents, which once again helped to cut costs.[16] Many of these landowners had not even been considering selling their land before Hardy approached them, but once Hardy had chosen a site, he was bound and determined to obtain it.[17]

He often learned about the landowners first, figuring out "what made them tick" before proposing the sale.[18] Sometimes he would convince the landowner that he or she would benefit by having a lumberyard nearby.[19] Sometimes he just used old-fashioned charisma and salesmanship. Bernie Magerko, Maggie Hardy Magerko's father-in-law, recalled one

Initially, 84 Lumber stores required just three to four acres of land, but as inventory grew to include home-improvement items and house-building kits, the company looked for 10-acre sites.

time when Hardy convinced an Oklahoma landowner to sell a parcel of land that had been in the family since the pioneer land grab of the 1800s.

"Joe... [doesn't] take no for an answer," Magerko said. "He goes over to this fellow that had the property, and he got what he wanted."[20]

Although the company performed studies to determine the suitability of potential sites, Hardy considered site selection more of an art than a science. On one trip throughout the western United States that became the stuff of 84 Lumber legend, employees joked that any town where Hardy stopped to use a restroom would eventually have an 84 Lumber store.[21] Bob Martik, who with his brother, Dean, built about 25 stores for the company remembered such an occasion.

"[Joe] wanted me to look at a house that [he] wanted to fix up a little or something," Martik said. "All of a sudden, he pulls off the road at the exit. ... [He] goes through the stop sign. People are blowing the horn. He just waves to them. Six months later, on that corner, there's a store."[22]

When Hardy heard about a potential site, he did not wait to investigate it. Ray Barley, one of 84 Lumber's regional managers, recalled that often

A 1978 ribbon-cutting ceremony celebrates the opening of a new 84 Lumber store. Employees remembered that openings could be hectic events, partly because of Joe Hardy's habit of moving up opening dates.

when he showed up to meet Hardy for a planning meeting on a Saturday morning, he would find himself being pulled along on a site-finding trip.

As Barley remembered it, Hardy would simply say, "Come here for a minute," and Barley would be whisked away for an entire day or even a weekend to look at a potential site in another city or state.[23]

Nick Ludi, who later became chief pilot for 84 Lumber, remembered that site selection trips were not for the faint of heart. "When Joe hits the road, it is all day and then some," Ludi said. "It will be two full days at least in one day. ... That's the way he does it. That's... his drive. He just keeps going and going and going."

Ludi recalled one occasion when Hardy had injured his knee but insisted on making his trip. "We couldn't carry him up the steps," Ludi said. "He had a cast or something on his leg. So we actually lifted him up. ... He was still out working when he should have been resting. [For Hardy], there is no such thing as resting."[24]

Jim Zaunick, who later worked as a civil engineer in 84 Lumber's real estate department, remembered that Hardy developed a love for Kentucky Fried Chicken, and it became the standard meal on site trips.

"So wherever you landed, you had to try to find KFC," Zaunick said. "If you couldn't, you had to find something... close. ... He loves his five pieces of white breast with his unsweetened ice tea, and his baked beans."

Whenever possible, Hardy would take advantage of the airport's courtesy car to avoid having to rent one. Most of them, Zaunick said, were of questionable quality. He recalled:

You look outside, and it's this beat up Chevy. So it's us four jumping in this beat up Chevy, and you turn it... and it starts. Boom ba-boom. It's got the exhaust thing. The windows don't work. You've got the felt from the ceiling on your head, and you're driving down the road, and you come to the stoplight, and it stalls out.

One time I remember... it was myself, him, and another site investigator and one of our attorneys. We get the rental car. We jump in the car. We're driving down the road. It's this white van. ... We're probably gone about an hour. ... We drive back. It's like, "Come on. Let's get going on the next trip." So we pull up ... and there's this lady standing outside with her arms folded. She's... staring at us. ... Well, here we stole her car. We had the wrong rental car. It was two vans parked next to each other, and we took hers instead.[25]

Hardy also began a tradition of conducting summer visits to check up on all his stores. Contract Sales Area Manager Greg Clark, who celebrated his 35th anniversary with the company in 2004, recalled the preparation that went into those annual visits:

We would work late at night polishing everything up, shining it all up. Mr. Hardy would then make his presence to do the inspection of the store. Almost like a military thing. Everyone was in their full dress, fresh haircuts, you know, standing at attention. ... Joe would walk through and talk to everybody and let us know how we were doing. Most of the time positive but sometimes negative. ... He always had a way of subtly making known that something wasn't correct without even saying anything about it.

High Expectations

Hardy was willing to work 80 hours a week, or more if needed, to make 84 Lumber a success, and he expected the same level of dedication from his associates. One way that this played out was with grand openings. When a new store was under construction, a grand opening schedule was always established. It would include a timeline and a projected date for the opening. Associates knew better than to tell Hardy that a store would not be ready by the projected date.

But even when everything was going according to plan, Hardy was not always satisfied. When work was being completed on schedule, he sometimes moved a grand opening up a couple of weeks, creating a crisis timeline.[26] Employees ended up working 24 hours a day during the final week before a grand opening to make sure that the store was ready, but they all preferred doing the hard work to telling Hardy that the store would not open on time.[27]

As usual, Hardy used these high-intensity situations as an opportunity to teach. Cecil Gravely recalled a time when, as a young man in his early 20s, he was responsible for having a store ready for its grand opening but was unable to get in touch with the plumber who was supposed to work on the bathrooms at the new location. Gravely told Hardy about his problem and received the following advice:

[Hardy] says, "I'll tell you what you do. In the morning, you get up at 4. You go to the plumber's house, and you [sit] on his doorstep, and when he comes out, you tackle him, and you ask him if he's going to plumb your bathrooms today, and I'll call you tomorrow to see how it turned out." Well... I got up at 4, and I was at his house at 5. When he [came] out of his house, I was there. I said, "Mr. whatever-your-name-is, I need you to plumb my bathrooms today because we have a deadline." He said, "Let's go do it."... I learned something there that's very important. You just have to make it happen. ... And you don't tell Joe, "I can't do it."[28]

Hardy refused to let even Mother Nature stand in the way of his store openings. Harry Zeune, who built several 84 Lumber stores, recalled a time when Hardy ordered him to pour a concrete foundation in near-zero temperatures in order to remain on sched-

ule.[29] However, Zeune also recalled that Hardy made it very clear that if for some reason the concrete did not set properly, it would be Zeune's fault![30]

84 Lumber required new recruits to prove themselves, and those who did often went on to have successful, long-term careers with the company. James Funyak, who worked for 84 Lumber for 30 years, remembered being hired to work "part time" at the Cresson, Pennsylvania, store. "Not part-time hours," he said, "just part-time status." Funyak's initiation to the company involved spending the entire summer painting the chain-link fence that surrounded the store.[31]

Jerry King, another long-time manager who joined 84 Lumber after serving in the Marine Corps, credited his military training with helping him to survive the first few months at the company.

"You opened the gates at 8:00 and basically ran all day long until 5:00, and you would send out for sandwiches... and eat in," King said. On the rare occasions when he was able to take a meal break, he said, it was "on the fly."[32]

As the years went by, Hardy's children also became more and more involved with the family business. Each of them worked for the company for at least a short while, and none of them got a free ride. 84 Lumber employees recalled that Hardy's children were expected to work just as hard as everyone else, and sometimes even harder.[33]

Barbara Stork, who began working at 84 Lumber in 1968, said that she had worked with all of the Hardy children at one time or another. "They were treated just like everyone else," she said. "They worked from the bottom up."[34]

The Hardy Way of Life

During the 1970s, Joe Hardy's son, Joe Jr., became a vice president of 84 Lumber. The job brought with it a demanding work schedule, and as the company expanded to locations throughout the United States, Joe Jr. was responsible for traveling to new stores and checking out their operations.

Joe Jr.'s son, Alex Hardy, accompanied his father on many of these trips, as well as grand openings and said that what he remembered most was the bare-bones budgets of the typical 84 Lumber business trip. As in all aspects of his business, Joe Hardy had mandated a no-frills approach to business travel

'84 U' HELPS MANAGERS EXCEL

IN ANY BUSINESS, CONTINUING EDUCA-tion is one key to remaining ahead of the competition. Joe Hardy realized the importance of employee education to ensure that his workers were able to give customers the best service possible.

Accordingly, a series of job training programs known as 84 University was developed to make sure that all 84 Lumber employees had the information they needed to excel at their jobs.

All associates were required to attend the once-a-year training, and Joe Hardy himself presided over the training sessions. Initially, a training area would be set up in a central location within driving distance of five or six 84 Lumber stores.[1] Associates would then drive in for an intensive one-day meeting.

Most of the time was spent receiving instruction in company policies and procedures, as well as in basic selling techniques and strategies.[2] There were also skills demonstrations in which employees learned how to read blueprints and repair damaged merchandise, and for a bit of fun there were 84 Lumber trivia games.[3]

Hardy enjoyed the sessions because it gave him a chance to meet with all of his employees once a year.[4] As the company grew, however, it became impractical for so many individual training sessions to be arranged.

Dan Hixenbaugh, who also provided training instruction, recalled, "It got too complicated for us. Joe wanted to be at every meeting, and when we got up to 300, 400 stores, we just couldn't do it. ... But it was great training for the kids. They saw Joe at his best. He'd rant and rave and yell about this or that, but it was very worthwhile, too."[5]

During the late 1970s, Hardy decided that a new system was needed, and he asked Jeanene Tomshay to design a more thorough employee training program.[6] Tomshay developed an eight-part home study course and served as

Jeanene Tomshay, left, shown here at her retirement party with Joe Hardy and Maggie Hardy Magerko, developed an 84 University home study course and went on to serve as the company's director of training. She was also vice president of advertising from 1981 to 1994.

84 Lumber's director of training for the next three years.[7]

Eventually, however, in the interest of reintroducing a more personal approach, a training center was built in Eighty Four, Pennsylvania, across the street from the original 84 Lumber warehouse. The center provided a venue for 84 Lumber managers from across the country to meet and learn the skills that would enhance their careers and benefit the company.

and at times went beyond the normal bounds of thriftiness to cut costs. Alex Hardy recalled:

Now if you remember anything about grand openings, they did not stay at the Broadmoor. They did not stay at the Carlton. ... First, they'd never sleep one guy to a room. It was always multiple guys in a room. ... It was the types of rooms and the types of locations where you'd go in, and you were surprised your car was still there the next morning.[35]

However, Joe Jr. worked tirelessly, crisscrossing the country to visit new locations, attend to problems and look for new ways to help 84 Lumber grow. He and his family moved frequently, almost every year, to remain close to the most important areas in the expanding 84 Lumber chain. Despite these frequent moves, Joe Jr. spent many days on the road, traveling from one location to the next.

At the time, 84 Lumber employees, including Joe Hardy, very seldom flew anywhere. He thought nothing of driving eight or 10 hours to avoid paying for an airplane ticket, or driving through the night so that he would not have to spend money on a motel room.

Joe Jr., for his part, had inherited his father's reckless driving skills, as well as his grit and determination. Alex Hardy recalled that on a few occasions out-of-state highway police showed up at the family home with arrest warrants for his father as a result of unpaid speeding tickets earned in the service of 84 Lumber.[36]

In every way possible, Joe Jr. threw himself into the job of making 84 Lumber a success. Alex Hardy recalled:

His world was 84. He traveled, I'm probably exaggerating, but as a young child, it seemed to me he was on the road for 45 weeks of the year, and when I say 45 weeks, I'm not talking Monday through Friday. I'm talking Monday through

Sunday. He was gone. ... And when he was home, he and my grandfather used to have competitions to see who could get to the office earlier, and I think the record was like 2 in the morning or it may be even 1 in the morning.[37]

Hardy's children and grandchildren recalled that both he and Joe Jr. showed a single-minded commitment to their work that could cut into family time. According to Alex Hardy:

[My father] and my grandfather were very similar in many, many different ways in their prime. I mean, very aggressive, very hard-working, and totally focused on the success of the company. My dad, his definition of success wasn't spending any time with us. His definition of success was, "I'm going to make these stores work," and that's what he did. It was never questioned. My mother didn't question it because she knew it wasn't a point of debate.[38]

At the same time, many aspects of the 84 Lumber business philosophy were incorporated in positive ways into the Hardy family life. Joe Hardy's daughter Robin Hardy Freed remembered that, as a child, she did not think of her father as a businessman, only

Joe Hardy Jr., right, shown here with son Alex Hardy, left, and grandson Sean, shared his father's dedication to 84 Lumber. Joe Jr. and his family moved frequently to remain close to critical areas of expansion, and he spent most of his time traveling to various stores to check up on their operations.

as being someone who was a great deal of fun. As she grew older, however, the lessons that Hardy drilled into all 84 Lumber employees became an important part of her own life, as well. One day, a countryside drive with her father led to a lesson that she would not soon forget. She remembered:

He and I were driving around somewhere, and I saw a little horse with a little foal running beside it, and I said, "Look at that. It's so beautiful just watching the two run through the hills of western Pennsylvania." About a week later, the foal was delivered to our house. ... Anyone can just appreciate the beauty of that horse running... but he didn't

just give you a gift without a lesson, and my lesson on that was I had to [work]. ... He bought me a book [about] how to train a horse. I'd never had a horse. Never been on a horse. The lesson was, you can see and appreciate the beauty. Now you have to learn about it, too.[39]

Alex Hardy also remembered his grandfather leading him around stores from an early age in order to teach him about 84 Lumber and the basic principles of business. For Joe Hardy, every interaction was an opportunity to teach the younger generation. His pride in his company was legendary among

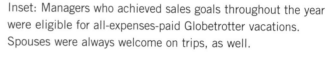

Inset: Managers who achieved sales goals throughout the year were eligible for all-expenses-paid Globetrotter vacations. Spouses were always welcome on trips, as well.

84 Lumber's Globetrotters travel incentive program was launched in 1972, when Joe Hardy rewarded his managers with a trip to Hawaii after the company reached $84 million in sales. Here, the Globetrotters enjoy sailing in St. Lucia.

Joe Hardy and Ed Ryan purchased The Meadows racetrack in Meadow Lands, Pennsylvania, after they got involved in harness racing but later sold it to Ladbrokes, a British company.

his employees and family members, and this was passed on to his managers, as well as his children.

Just Rewards

Although many employees enjoyed the excitement and constant change provided by life at 84 Lumber, the nonstop pace and all-consuming schedule was not for everyone. After nearly 20 years of working in the lumber business with his brother, Bob Hardy decided to leave 84 Lumber in 1974. He had served as company president up until that time[40] and looked back fondly on his years with 84 Lumber.[41]

Reflecting on his feelings about 84 Lumber when the company first began, he remarked, "We just felt it would be successful. We just felt it. I don't know why. It was probably the wrong thing to do, but we just felt we'd stick together, and we'd be fine."[42]

Bob Hardy went on to pursue a career in harness racing, taking part in a sport that had become very important to his brother Joe as well.[43] Joe Hardy and Ed Ryan had purchased The Meadows racetrack in Meadow Lands, Pennsylvania, about seven miles from Eighty-Four. Bob Hardy used to go to the track to watch races and training sessions and had such a good time that he eventually decided to make racing his profession.[44]

Ryan experimented with buying thoroughbred horses for a time, and he and Hardy greatly enjoyed their time at the racetrack.[45] They became close friends with Delvin Miller, a harness racing legend and founder of the track. Ed Ryan and Joe Hardy's old friend Peter Cameron even experimented with driving horses in the races, but Hardy preferred to cheer from the stands.[46] The venture was not a financial success, however, and was eventually sold to the British company Ladbrokes.[47]

For Dottie Hardy, on the other hand, harness racing became a lifelong passion that was ignited when she acquired her first horse, *Snibbor*, her father Robbins Pierce's first name spelled backward. Over the years, Dottie became well-known in racing circles across the country as a top-level breeder and owner, and in 1981, her champion horse *Delmonica Hanover* competed in the prestigious Prix d'Amerique in France.[48]

Joe Hardy was not the only person at 84 Lumber who was able to take time off and enjoy himself in this way. While Hardy demanded devotion and hard work from his employees, he responded with rewards for those who were equal to the task. Hardy developed a multilayered system of goals and incentives for all his workers.

Each store in the 84 Lumber chain, for example, had certain sales goals for the month. If they met their goal, the employees would receive cash bonuses.[49] Hardy was a master motivator and used this strategy to make sure that his workers felt that they, too, were reaping the benefits of 84 Lumber's success.

At the same time, he never lost track of the larger issues essential to running his business. Gail

Baughman, for example, recalled that one month he "bent" his sales figures to make it appear that his store had reached its sales quota for the month so that his workers could receive their bonus.[50] One of his employees reported him to Joe Hardy. When Hardy called Baughman into his office, however, Hardy did not ask why Baughman had altered the figures, but rather why Baughman had an employee who was willing to turn him in.[51]

Baughman replied, "I don't know. I never liked that guy, and I don't talk to him much." Joe Hardy responded with his trademark combination of temper and wisdom, screaming "If you can't even talk to them, they shouldn't be working for you."[52]

Baughman was sent back to work with not only the motivation to make sure he made his quota the following month, but with a valuable lesson in manager/employee relations, as well.[53]

Another system that Hardy used to reward his employees was a generous pension plan. Stock options and profit sharing were some other early incentives.[54] Later on, he developed a plan whereby 84 Lumber would put 84 cents into a retirement account for every dollar invested by an employee.[55]

One popular incentive for long-term service was the Ten Year Club, a program that provided a party or weekend retreat for all employees who had spent 10 years or more with 84 Lumber. While Hardy was a part owner of The Meadows, Ten Year Club events were often held during the *Adios* stakes races, the racetrack's biggest event of the year. Ten Year Club members watched the race while enjoying a luxury luncheon at a trackside restaurant.

Another unforgettable Ten Year Club event was a 1979 "Roman Orgy" party held at Joe Hardy's home that was complete with heaps of Italian food and a toga contest, for which the grand prize was a trip to the small town of Rome, New York.[56] Such programs helped promote worker loyalty and ensure that employees spent many years with 84 Lumber.

Ed Ryan experimented with harness racing, but Joe Hardy preferred to cheer from the stands. Dottie Hardy, on the other hand, became known as a top-level owner and breeder of race horses, including the champion *Delmonica Hanover*. (Photo courtesy of U. S. Trotting Association)

"I think if you could describe the company in three basic statements, it's people, incentives, and systems," said Frank Cicero, who worked his way up from co-manager of 84 Lumber's Seabrook, Maryland, store to company vice president for store operations. "You know, hire great people, have great people working for you. We have incentives that drive people and put systems in place to help people."[57]

Although the other rewards were a hit, the Globetrotters travel program was the most popular by far. In 1972, Joe Hardy promised his managers that if the company as a whole reached $84 million in sales for the year they would all take a trip to Hawaii.[58] With such a tempting target, the managers did their utmost to reach the sales record, and they were successful.

In the years that followed, Hardy continued the tradition of providing all-expenses-paid group vacations to managers who reached certain sales goals throughout the year and to their spouses. The travelers became known as the Globetrotters and visited locations across the United States and throughout the world.

These incentives were apparently effective; 84 Lumber opened 229 stores during the 1970s

Above: 84 Lumber associates kick up their heels at a party for the Ten Year Club. *(Photo by Michael Redford)*

Below: Joe Hardy and Pete Cameron, left, were close friends throughout their lives, and the two men often consulted each other on business decisions. Hardy also admired Cameron's quirky sense of humor, recalling a time when Cameron found a snake on a golf course and put it in Hardy's bag as a joke.

Joe Hardy's 1979 Roman Orgy party was a hit with employees, who were still talking about the event many years later. Bud and Helen Dolfi said the party was so memorable because of little details that added to the fun, such as the Leaning Tower of Pisa centerpieces, the torches that lined Hardy's driveway, and an enormous salad bowl built from miniature rolls.

alone and reached annual revenues of $426 million by 1979.[59]

Challenges and Opportunities

Perhaps the greatest motivator of all, however, was not an official program, but the sense of independence and responsibility with which Hardy imbued his employees. Thinking back on their years of service with the company, many remarked that working at 84 Lumber had afforded them opportunities that they would not have received elsewhere.

"Joe is always one to test you, and even when you get comfortable in a situation and think you have all the ins and outs figured out, he'll very quickly change you or put you into a new setting to learn a new [skill]... and it's good," Ray Barley recalled.[60]

Similarly Bud Weber, a manager who spent more than three decades with the company, said, "In working with Joe and Maggie... they afford you the opportunity to do what you want, as fast as you want, and achieve any level that you want. There are no... restrictions on how far you can go with 84. ... If you want to try something, you're given the opportunity. Around here, you're given the opportunity to succeed, not to fail."[61]

Bill Underdonk, who worked as a salesman and manager for 84 Lumber for 36 years, compared Hardy to a great athletic coach. He said, "The ones that you remember are the ones that kind of edged you a little bit and made you think a little bit, and maybe you didn't like it then, and about five years down the road, you loved it."[62]

But while Hardy demanded excellence of his associates, he never required perfection. He did expect, however, that his employees learn from their errors. Cheri Bomar, corporate counsel and vice president of development, remarked, "Mr. Hardy always likes to say, 'I don't care if you make a mistake, but let's make different mistakes than the old ones. I want to hear new challenges.'"[63]

Cap Moore, who worked at 84 Lumber for nearly 30 years, added, "I had no education. I just finished high school. And I went [on to be] the president of the Western Division. ... There was just no limit to what [Joe Hardy] would let you do if you wanted to."[64]

Dan Wallach, another long-time employee, noted that he learned early on not to approach Joe with a problem without first determining the best solution. "You should always come in with a solution, and I learned to tell him the solution before you say the problem."[65]

Several of Hardy's associates also remembered him as unfailingly loyal to the employees who had spent years working for him. Virginia Hackman, whose husband, Bob, set up 84 Lumber's real estate

84 Lumber associates enjoy another Globetrotters rewards trip to Maui in 1984. Employees said the vacations were wonderful, but the greatest motivator of all was Joe Hardy's belief in their ability to handle challenges and responsibility.

department, said that when Bob experienced a sudden illness, Hardy provided him with what he needed to work at home.[66]

And Nancy Young, whose deceased husband, Dave, was a long-time friend of Hardy and ran 84's purchasing deparment for many years, said her husband was honored to be the only person outside the Hardy family to receive stock in the company.[67]

For his part, Hardy believed that his employees were able to achieve great things because he believed that the key to business success was in tapping the power of the individual. He said:

I believe in the power of teamwork... but there's a greater power, and that greater power is the power of the individual. It's like when I had the racetrack, I asked this guy how he was so successful in driving horses. He said, "Joe, I keep a light rein. I let the horse have its head. It has more brains how he can get through the pack than I do."[68]

During the 1980s, Joe Hardy focused on an ambitious expansion plan for 84 Lumber that included reaching out to more high-end consumers. The effort was not profitable, however, and Hardy learned that the strength of his company lay in keeping things simple.

CHAPTER SEVEN

84 RETURNS TO ITS ROOTS

This is what makes the company, makes the man. ... You have to make tough decisions. You have to make unpopular decisions.

—Joe Hardy, founder of 84 Lumber

AS THE 1980s DAWNED, JOE Hardy was busy taking advantage of new methods of expanding and advertising his company. In 1980, 84 Lumber produced its first television show, a do-it-yourself home repair program called *Helpful How-To's.*[1]

The show was aired on Pittsburgh's KDKA television station, as well as on a station in Indianapolis, Indiana, and featured 84 Lumber employee Don Fico as "Mr. Goodcarpenter."[2] The 13-week series helped increase public awareness of 84 Lumber and allowed the company to enlarge its customer base.[3]

This foray into the world of television, however, was only a small part of Hardy's plans for 84 Lumber. During this decade, Hardy plotted an aggressive expansion program that he hoped would propel 84 Lumber through the next 10 years. Hardy decided that 1984, the company's "signature" year, was an ideal time to put his plans into action and began carrying out his $1 billion plan to upgrade and expand the 84 Lumber chain.

84 Lumber had grown from its humble beginnings in Eighty Four, Pennsylvania, to be the nation's sixth-largest building supply retailer.[4] The company was comprised of 374 stores in 38 states and was adding new locations every year.[5]

Hardy hoped that within 10 years he could make 84 Lumber the largest building supply company in the United States.[6] He had to contend with huge chains such as The Home Depot and No. 1-ranked Lowe's, and he began to look to these companies for ideas as to how he could modify 84 Lumber to increase the company's profits.

One change was to improve the stores themselves. Traditionally, 84 Lumber stores featured minimalist construction, with concrete floors covered by rows upon rows of lumber racks.

"The [employees] didn't care a whole lot about the appearance of their building, neither inside nor out," said Phil Drake, who worked on the renovations. "In their minds, they were selling lumber, so what did it matter?" However, he said, "when you walked in as a customer, you had no idea where anything was unless you went there every day. They didn't even have things priced at that time. You had to walk up to the front desk and [ask]."[7]

As part of his improvement plan, Hardy allotted $100 million to upgrade existing stores, adding additional lighting and bright vinyl flooring, among other improvements.[8]

Maggie Hardy became president of her father's Nemacolin Woodlands Resort when she was 21 years old and spent the next several years demonstrating that she also had the skills to run 84 Lumber.

He hoped that these remodeled stores would attract more high-end customers, but he was taking a gamble by departing from the no-frills approach that had worked so well for 84 Lumber through the years.

The expansion plan also included the addition of 330 new 84 Lumber stores over the course of seven years.[9] In 1984 alone, there were plans to open 30 new 84 Lumber locations.[10] Many of the new stores were to be introduced in urban areas, another tactic designed to attract more upscale customers.[11]

This approach again diverged from 84 Lumber's traditional rural focus, and subjected the company to strenuous market-share competition with larger retailers who already had stores in those areas.

The expansion strategy was the most risky part of Hardy's new business plan. In 1984, 84 Lumber had only $1 million in long-term debt, an insignificant amount for a company of its size.[12] In order to finance the expansion, Hardy would have to take on $300 million in long-term debt, sell some of his land holdings, and sell and re-lease many existing 84 Lumber stores.[13] Hardy was enthusiastic about the plan, however, and launched it full-force, as he did all his business ventures, without looking back.

Initially, the plan appeared successful, as new stores opened and existing stores were renovated. Spirits were high as the company celebrated "The Year of '84" in various ways. The 84th customer at the store in Eighty Four, Pennsylvania, on the 84th day of the year (March 24) was awarded a cash prize.[14] The United States Post Office granted the home offices in Eighty Four their own zip code, 15384.[15] Several new 84 Lumber stores experienced record sales at their grand openings.[16]

Also in 1984, Joe Hardy was awarded an honorary Doctorate of Laws from Washington and Jefferson University.[17] Three years later, Hardy would establish a program for the study and encouragement of entrepreneurship at the same university.[18]

Meanwhile, other 84 Lumber programs that had been in place for some time started to gain national attention. One of these was the sale of prepackaged home-building kits, which included all the lumber and trim needed to build a home, with the foundation, wiring, plumbing, and heating systems purchased separately.[19] All pieces were labeled and mapped out on a blueprint, and the houses were designed so that anyone with basic carpentry skills and a few helpers could assemble them.[20]

Left: In 1984, the company's "signature year," the U.S. Post Office granted the home offices in Eighty Four, Pennsylvania, their own zip code—15384.

Opposite top: 84 Lumber's prepackaged home-building kits, which included all the lumber and trim needed to build a home, attracted publicity for the company and allowed people with basic construction skills to build a home for about half of its market value.

Opposite right: 84 Lumber associates in Brookpark, Ohio, celebrate record grand opening sales. During the 1980s, Joe Hardy developed a $1 billion expansion plan that called for the opening of 330 new stores and $100 million in upgrades to existing stores.

Designs ranged from small, single-story homes to the two-story "Plantation" model for more advanced builders[21] and were manufactured in a plant in Victor, New York.[22] People who opted to use the kits could build a home for about half of its market value.[23] Several newspapers across the country featured stories about local residents who had built their homes using 84 Lumber kits, and the publicity helped the company to draw more customers.

A Difficult Decision

However, 84 Lumber failed to meet its sales goals that year, delaying renovations for many stores.[24] In addition, several things occurred that called the future of the company into doubt, one of

the most critical of which involved the future leadership of 84 Lumber. For years, many 84 Lumber employees had assumed that Joe Hardy Jr. would eventually take over control of the company from his father.

Joe Jr.'s son Alex Hardy recalled that, for his father, "the business was pleasure, and he didn't view it ever as business."[25]

Joe Jr. demonstrated a drive and commitment to the company that rivaled his father's, and he was fully committed to the success of 84 Lumber. At times, however, this dedication was as much a disadvantage as it was an asset.

The two men, both strong-willed and determined, often clashed over business decisions and competed in demonstrating their commitments to the company. Joe Jr. was giving 84 Lumber all he had, but unfortunately, circumstances beyond his control would lead to the end of his career at 84 Lumber.

During the early 1980s, Joe Jr. began to suffer from various ailments. He eventually developed Bell's palsy, a paralysis of the facial nerve.[26] In 1985, doctors diagnosed Joe Jr. with multiple sclerosis, also known as MS. The disease is caused by scar tissue in the central nervous system and leads to reduced neurological function.[27] Some people with MS experience very minor symptoms, or MS "attacks," for several years after diagnosis, which are sometimes followed by partial or complete recovery.[28]

After his diagnosis, Joe Jr. decided to take a six-month sabbatical from 84 Lumber in the hopes that his health would improve. Even during that time, he insisted on remaining involved with the company, but he was not able to maintain his customary intense involvement in day-to-day operations.[29]

After his sabbatical, Joe Jr. returned to 84 Lumber and began working his hectic schedule again, but it proved too heavy a workload. The reduced stamina and fatigue caused by his disease made it impossible for Joe Jr. to work the 12-hour days, early morning shifts, and cross-country trips that he was used to and which his father demanded of an 84 Lumber assistant president.

As time passed, Joe Hardy became increasingly dissatisfied with the work his son was doing, and Joe Jr. found that his illness was preventing him from devoting as much time as he would have liked to 84 Lumber.

Finally, in 1988, Joe Hardy asked his son to leave the company. The decision was a difficult one, on which Hardy reflects, "This is what makes the company, makes the man. ... You have to make tough decisions. You have to make unpopular decisions."[30]

Alex Hardy recalled that his father, Joe Jr., was devastated by the move. "Love is not even the right word to describe what my father felt for 84..." he said. "It was his entire life. He threw everything he had at it until he got sick. He gave everything he had."[31]

Joe Jr. took a year off work to cope with his illness and think about the direction he wanted his life to take. Then he showed that he had unquestionably inherited the Hardy spirit of determination.

In 1989, he started his own business, Hardy Enterprises, a construction and real estate development company.[32] Since that time, his MS has remained largely in remission.[33] In 1999, Alex Hardy joined the business and took over day-to-day operations.[34] Hardy Enterprises also created a spin-off business, S&T Commercial Construction.[35]

'Nothing Fancy'

As the 1980s progressed, it became apparent that Hardy's ambitious expansion plan was not entirely successful. The overhaul had led to some positive changes, however.

In 1987, for example, 84 Lumber started offering credit for the first time.[36] This was a huge departure from the strict cash-and-carry policy that had made the company a success, but it was necessary to attract business from contractors and other building professionals.[37] 84 Lumber locations also began leasing trucks and providing delivery and job-site order services.[38]

Other aspects of the plan did not work so well. Some of the new store locations did not have a large enough customer base to generate profits, and others suffered from too much competition with other retailers. The company had overextended itself, and many of the new stores were eventually forced to close.[39]

Furthermore, the cosmetic improvements to 84 Lumber stores and the additional product lines had attracted some new customers, but they had also greatly increased the company's overhead costs.[40] Sales increased, but profits did not rise in proportion.[41]

In the years that followed, Hardy would refer to the 1980s as his "sleeping time," a time when he felt he did not make the best decisions for his company.[42] He found that his efforts to attract the casual, do-it-yourself customers had hurt the company, and he decided to refocus on attracting professional builders as the chain's primary clientele.[43]

Hardy had made some mistakes, but he had also learned a valuable lesson: that the strength of his company lay in keeping things simple.

Looking back on the era several years later, Hardy remarked, "Every time we varied from that approach... we got into trouble. We have to constantly remind ourselves of what we are. We deal in commodities—basic building products, nothing fancy."[44]

A New Passion

Despite these setbacks, Joe Hardy was not one to let himself be dragged down. In 1987, at the age of 64, he embarked on what would become a new driving passion in his life, an all-consuming project that would demand almost as much of his attention as 84 Lumber had.

The entire project was launched with a simple desire to buy a present for his daughter Maggie. She and Hardy often took fishing trips together, and he had decided to buy a piece of land with a pond where Maggie could fish whenever she liked.

He heard about a land auction to be held at the Nemacolin Trails Hunting Reserve, located about

Top: Family members and 84 Lumber associates said that Joe and Maggie Hardy were able to work together so effectively because she had the ability to fight for what she believed was best for the company without locking horns with her father.

Center: Nemacolin Woodlands Resort is located in Pennsylvania's Laurel Highlands, which was once a popular vacation spot for wealthy residents of Pittsburgh. *(Photo courtesy of Nemacolin Woodlands Resort and Spa)*

Right: When Joe Hardy attended the auction for the Nemacolin property, he had simply been interested in buying a fishing pond for his daughter Maggie. Later, amenities at the resort would include fishing, boating, and canoeing. *(Photo courtesy of Nemacolin Woodlands Resort and Spa)*

50 miles from Eighty Four in Farmington, Pennsylvania, and made plans to attend.

The Nemacolin area was named for Chief Nemacolin, a leader of the Lanai Lanape Indians,[45] who blazed a trail through the Laurel Highland mountains in 1740.[46] That path was later used by George Washington and General Edward Braddock during the French and Indian War, and it was eventually expanded into a highway.[47]

During the 1800s, the Laurel Highlands became a popular getaway for wealthy Pittsburghers, and the tradition continued into the 20th century.[48] The parcel of land that Hardy was considering had been purchased by Pittsburgh industrialist Willard Rockwell in 1968 for use as a private game reserve.[49]

Rockwell built a hunting lodge, airstrip, and golf course on the land and also added two lakes before selling the property to Cordelia Mellon Scaife, a member of two of Pittsburgh's most prominent families, in 1979.[50] Scaife used the area as an upscale corporate conference center before selling the property back to Rockwell in 1982.[51]

Rockwell, however, found that he could not afford to properly maintain the property,[52] and the 550 acres were eventually divided into several small parcels to be put up for sale at the bankruptcy auction Hardy was to attend.[53]

On the day of the auction, Hardy was running late. He asked his old friend Pete Cameron to accompany him to the sale, and the two sped down the highway to the auction.[54] The property was being offered for sale as one piece or in parcels,[55] and in the excitement of the auction, Hardy forgot his plan to buy a pond and decided to purchase the entire estate.[56]

He told the auctioneer of his intentions and was informed that he needed either a certified check or a letter from a financial institution stating that

Joe Hardy receives a key to the Nemacolin Woodlands Resort shortly after purchasing it for $3.1 million in 1987. Hardy said he bought the property because, after his success in building the 84 Lumber empire, he was ready for a new challenge.

he had sufficient funds to purchase the land.[57] Hardy, who had come to the auction more or less on a whim, had neither, and the auctioneer was unimpressed when Hardy attempted to use his famous name as a guarantee of his financial worth.[58]

However, nearby homeowners were anxious to see the Nemacolin property sold as one unit rather than divided into farms and other small plots.[59] Hardy asked the auctioneer to delay the sale while he drove to a bank in nearby Uniontown, Pennsylvania, for a certified check, and the auctioneer agreed.[60]

Nan Cameron, who accompanied Hardy and her husband to the sale, recalled that as they left the bank Pete Cameron spotted a roadside snack cart and insisted on grabbing a couple of hot dogs so that they would not have to sit through the entire auction without having had lunch.[61] Hardy spent one dollar, the only cash he had with him, to purchase the hot dogs, and as Nan Cameron recalled, he arrived at the auction in a mustard-covered shirt.[62]

However, he was successful in obtaining all the property and the Nemacolin lodge for $3.1 million.[63] What had started out as a fishing trip had become a project that would occupy both Joe and Maggie Hardy for many years to come.

Vision Becomes Reality

When Hardy purchased Nemacolin, he had no idea what he wanted to do with it. He bought it simply for something to do.

Hardy said, "At 64 [years old], I thought, 'Gee, I've enjoyed the lumber. Enjoyed the travel. Enjoyed being connected with it, but is there anything else?' At 64, some people are thinking of retiring. Well, no, my thought was, 'Is there anything else?' "[64]

It did not take long for Hardy to begin formulating plans for Nemacolin. After taking a good look at his newly purchased property he began brainstorming ideas for ways to make Nemacolin into a world-class resort.

The auction had taken place on a Friday. The following Monday, Hardy called developer Craig Johnson and asked him to come out to Farmington to look at Nemacolin and begin planning changes. 84 Lumber employees recalled that Hardy held a Ten-Year Club retreat at Nemacolin a week after the property was purchased. At the time, the hunting lodge was the only building at the resort, but Hardy walked his associates through the property, explaining all the developments he had in mind.

84 Lumber employee Bob MacKinney recalled that he was amazed at how quickly Hardy brought these elaborate plans to fruition.

"I mean it happens," MacKinney said. "It's just not somebody talking and nothing happening... he makes it happen. It's just ingenious, his dreams, and what he sees, and before you know it, it's reality."[65]

By the time another week had passed, Hardy had bulldozers on site, moving dirt.[66] By September, three months after the auction, construction had begun on a 10,000-square-foot conference center,[67] and a spa, golf course, and golf academy were soon to follow.[68] The initial construction at Nemacolin lasted five years, between 1987 and 1992, and Johnson oversaw all the design and development.[69]

The project naturally created many new jobs in the area, and some contractors were willing to go to great lengths to get work at Nemacolin. Don Gearhart, a developer with Penn Development Services, adopted Hardy's habit of investigating his "target" before trying to get a job.[70]

He learned that Hardy started each day at Nemacolin with an early morning visit to the spa. Gearhart determined to wait outside the spa until Hardy emerged and then introduce himself and see if there was any work for his company at Nemacolin.[71] He recalled:

I introduced myself to him and told him that I understand you're going to build a golf course, and we'd like to be considered for this type of work for just the major earth-moving portion of the golf course. He was listening to me and getting into his car, and I had him a little bit half-blocked where he was parked. He kind of gave me a nod and said, "Well, somebody will be in touch with you, and get out of the way before I run over you."[72]

Gearhart's grit was just the type of attitude that Hardy liked, however, and he was later hired to do the earth-moving work for the golf course. There was plenty of work to go around. During the first five years, Hardy invested $55 million of his own money in the project, constructing buildings, moving land, and working to build a reputation for Nemacolin Woodlands Resort as one of the country's premiere resorts.[73]

Of course, running 84 Lumber was still Joe Hardy's priority. In order to balance his two passions, he put his daughter Maggie Hardy, who was only 21 years old at the time, in charge of Nemacolin Woodlands Resort. She proved a capable overseer, and her father began to consider more seriously her potential as a businesswoman.

The Heir Apparent

After Joe Hardy Jr. left 84 Lumber, Joe Hardy had spent a great deal of time thinking about who would inherit his company. His younger son, Paul, had his own career in real estate and did not wish to run 84 Lumber.[74] Hardy also considered bringing Jack Shewmaker, former vice chairman of Wal-Mart, on board, but the two never established a partnership.[75]

The challenge of finding a new leader for the company was complicated by the fact that the identity of 84 Lumber was tied so strongly to Hardy himself.[76] Gail Baughman, one of the company's most senior employees, often remarked that he "consider[ed] himself working for Joe Hardy, not 84 Lumber."[77]

Hardy began to realize that the best person for the job was someone who had been involved with 84 Lumber since she had first learned how to walk. There were very few women who held executive positions in the lumber industry, but Maggie Hardy had been learning how to run 84 Lumber since she was a toddler.

Family members and 84 Lumber employees recall that while Joe Hardy and Joe Jr. often locked horns over business decisions, Maggie Hardy was able to handle her father and diffuse tensions while still holding her own as a strong-willed businesswoman. Father and daughter had developed a bond from Maggie's childhood days that was even stronger than the ones Hardy had with his other children, and it became an asset in their business dealings.

Joe and Maggie Hardy, shown here in front of their home, had always shared a special bond. During the 1980s, it became clear that they also shared the same spirit, drive, and commitment toward propelling 84 Lumber into a future filled with opportunity and change.

Joe Hardy's associates were amazed at how quickly his vision for the Nemacolin property as a world-class resort became reality. The initial phase of construction lasted just five years, but the $55 million project created many new jobs for contractors in the area. *(Photo courtesy of Nemacolin Woodlands Resort and Spa)*

As the years passed, Hardy gave Maggie increased responsibilities, and she became the new vice president of the company.

Reflecting on his relationship with his daughter, Hardy remarked, "Maggie and I have a certain thing. She's female. I'm male. But I'd say you'll never see two people [who are so much] the same."[78]

In the years to come, Maggie Hardy would prove that she did indeed share her father's drive and spirit, and together they would lead 84 Lumber into the coming decades and through all the changes those times would bring.

In 1992, Maggie Hardy assumed the title of president of 84 Lumber and took over the company's daily operations. *(Photo by Michael Redford)*

CHAPTER EIGHT

PASSING THE TORCH

I came along, and Dad didn't have a successor. I was sitting in the board-room, and they were talking about having to sell the company, and I said, "Give me a shot."

—Maggie Hardy Magerko, president of 84 Lumber

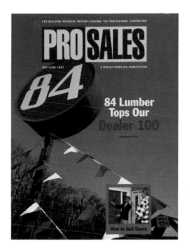

DURING THE 1990s, A MORE mature 84 Lumber began to emerge. In 1991, for example, 84 Lumber topped *Pro Sales* magazine's "Dealer 100" list, and by 1997, the company was ranked as No. 1 in pro sales by the building materials magazine *National Home Center News.*

Despite an unstable economic climate, the company continued to grow. From 1990 to 1991, for example, when housing starts were at record lows and the building industry as a whole suffered losses, 84 Lumber's total sales increased 11 percent.[1]

Several significant changes in company policy helped the company remain competitive throughout the decade. In 1995, 84 Lumber extended its credit program, and as a result its accounts receivable doubled.[2]

For old-timers like Jim McCorkle, who rose to the position of collection manager for 84 Lumber, taking credit was almost like "heresy" to the company built on the cash-and-carry concept. However, he said, "In order to be successful inside of 84, there's one thing you have to be, and that's adaptive. You have to be able to adapt to change and channel your focus... wherever the ship is being steered at the current point."[3]

The company also changed its sales focus. When big-box retailers began taking a large chunk of the walk-in, do-it-yourself market, 84 Lumber decided to focus more on sales to professional builders.[4]

84 Lumber also began a new campaign to market its prepackaged home kits, an effort dubbed "Affordable Homes Across America." The company filmed a 30-second television commercial to help promote the home kits and aired it during prime-time television shows.[5] Soon after that, a team of 84 Lumber employees was answering hundreds of calls a day from prospective homebuyers.[6]

The newly designed prepackaged homes cost between $39,900 and $69,900, and upgrade kits including garages, decks, or fireplaces could be purchased at additional cost.[7] Hardy set up a plant to manufacture the kits in Homestead, Florida,[8] where Hurricane Andrew struck in 1992, leaving a quarter-million Dade County residents temporarily homeless.[9]

At the same time, 84 Lumber was continuing to open new stores. In 1997, the company opened its 400th store, in Ephrata, Pennsylvania. Former Philadelphia Eagles quarterback Ron Jaworski

In 1991, 84 Lumber topped *Pro Sales* magazine's "Dealer 100" list, one of several national recognitions for the company during the 1990s. *(Photo courtesy of Hanley Wood Magazines)*

served as celebrity guest, and more than 2,000 visitors attended the grand opening.[10]

Despite these successes, Joe Hardy did not forget the foundation upon which the company had been built: his employees. In the early 1990s, Hardy decided to build a training center in Eighty Four, where employees from Pennsylvania and surrounding states could go to receive management training.

The center was christened the George T. Handyside Training Center in memory of George Handyside, 84's vice president of operations analysis who died suddenly in April 1991.[11] The facility was located across the road from the original 84 Lumber warehouse, and a two-story dormitory was constructed next to the training center to house manager trainees during their six-day training program.[12]

The new center opened on November 17, 1991.[13] Although several hundred employees a year would experience the program, they attended the seminars in small groups. The focus of the program was to get employees to think as entrepreneurs and future managers. Each day of the six-day course was devoted to one of six topics: 84 Lumber history and culture, selling skills, business knowledge, product knowledge, computer training, or motivational techniques.

According to Vice President of Store Operations Frank Cicero, 84 Lumber recognized the importance of individual managers to the company's overall success.

The George T. Handyside Training Center, which opened in 1991, included conference facilities and a dormitory to house manager trainees during their six-day training session.

The key... is finding the right store manager. When you have the right... manager, you cannot relax, but that one individual makes the biggest

difference. ... We had a store in Leesburg, Florida, and it was closed in the late '80s. We reopened it in '91 and put a store manager in there named Dan Stinton, and today, we've relocated the store from Leesburg to Tavares, and he'll do $41 million. It's the largest store in our company, and the bulk of that is [due] to that store manager because he's the guy that's there every day, building the team.[14]

Jim Guest joined 84 Lumber as a manager trainee in 1976 and was promoted through the ranks to director of associate development for the entire company. Guest said the training also helped young recruits to understand just how much they could accomplish at 84 Lumber simply by working hard. He told them, "the best example I can give you of how successful you can be is me."[15]

A New—But Experienced—Leader

An instrumental force in all this change was Maggie Hardy. After becoming executive vice president at 84 Lumber and president of Nemacolin Woodlands Resort, she spent five years proving to her father that she had the skills to handle the company.[16]

Although she had grown up with 84 Lumber, Maggie Hardy said she still had a lot to learn about managing and motivating employees. She said that, at first, she tried to emulate her father's management style but only managed to come off as obnoxious.

Maggie Hardy recalled that after she conducted an employee orientation at Nemacolin Woodlands Resort, one of her recent hires decided she didn't want to work for the company after all.

She told me the reason why she quit was me and how belligerent I was with people and didn't respect them. From that moment, I changed because... I didn't realize how offensive I was becoming. So after that, I cleaned up my act a little bit and really tried to understand more the people aspect of it.[17]

In 1992, when Maggie Hardy was 26 years old, Joe Hardy announced a formal handover of the company to his daughter.[18]

She recalled, "I came along, and Dad didn't have a successor. I was sitting in the boardroom, and they were talking about having to sell the company, and I said, 'Give me a shot.'"[19]

Joe Hardy had passed 40 percent of the company stock over to Maggie in 1991, and he added another 40 percent in 1992.[20] In addition to the tax benefits that he and his family reaped by making the transfer before he died, Joe Hardy also felt that putting Maggie clearly in charge of the company would reassure employees who might be worried about what would happen to 84 Lumber as Hardy grew older.[21]

And indeed, 84 Lumber associates appreciated having someone in charge who had worked

Joe Hardy believed it was important for employees to see a clear transition of leadership from himself to his daughter Maggie.

her way up through the company. Former 84 Lumber employee Terry Carter remarked:

> *Maggie knows every facet of 84 Lumber. She knows because she did it. She worked in the store. She realizes what it's like. ... You know, you have five deliveries to go out, and you have one forklift bro-*

Above: Maggie Hardy instructs employees during a training session. Seminars focused on topics such as 84 Lumber history and culture, sales, business skills, product knowledge, computers, and motivational techniques.

Right: Maggie Hardy poses with a group of associates at the company's training center.

ken down and one sitting there out of gas. She understands. It's what has kept her feet on the ground.[22]

With the second transfer of stock, Maggie Hardy also assumed the title of president of 84 Lumber and took over the company's day-to-day operations, leaving her father more time to concentrate on special projects and on the selection of new 84 Lumber store sites.[23]

Maggie Hardy recalled that the transition was so successful because she had the help of mentors like Denny Brua, who spent 27 years at 84 Lumber. She said:

> *[Denny] allowed me to get into the company without anyone feeling threatened or nervous about the security of their jobs. I don't even know how he did it. Just a very nice flow with it. I mean he put me under his wing and taught me a lot of things that maybe my dad didn't.*[24]

But Joe Hardy, as well as 84 Lumber employees, said the successful transition was mostly due to Maggie's willingness to put her intelligence, experience, and people skills to use in earning the respect of her workers.

Recalling that his daughter had once dreamed of being a social worker when she grew up, Joe Hardy said, "Empathy is a big word you'd have to

LORD HARDY

NOT CONTENT WITH OWNING A BLOSsoming luxury resort and a lumber business worth hundreds of millions of dollars, in 1990 Joe Hardy decided to take a foray into the world of royalty.

While on a trip to England he heard by chance about an auction of royal titles.[1] Several titles, most of them of purely ceremonial value, were to be sold, and Hardy could not resist attending the event.[2]

He ended up buying the title of Lord of the Manor of Henley-in-Arden, a small town in Warwickshire, England. The price of this illustrious title was a mere £93,500 (approximately $168,300) and brought with it several perks.[3]

As Lord of the Manor, Hardy was authorized to hold weekly markets in Henley-in-Arden, to lead processions and events such as the Henley Mop Fair, and to use the manorial coat of arms on his letterhead.[4] He could also preside over Henley Leet, the town's annual manorial court session.[5]

Hardy's newfound nobility gave rise to what would become one of western Pennsylvania's highest-profile social events, the Royal Reception at Nemacolin Woodlands Resort.

On the first anniversary of receiving his title, Hardy held the first Royal Reception to mark the occasion, with former British Prime Minister Edward Heath as the guest of honor.[6] Dignitaries from Henley-in-Arden were also flown in for the ceremony, and 900 guests attended.[7]

As the years went by, the notable names on the special guest list for the Royal Reception grew. *Lifestyles of the Rich and Famous* host Robin Leach and actresses Eva Gabor and Lynn Redgrave were just a few of the famous guests.[8]

In 1995, Hardy decided to bequeath his title to his daughter Robin Hardy Freed. A special ceremony was conducted at the annual Royal Reception in order to transfer the title, and comedienne Joan Rivers served as the emcee.

Hardy declared his desire to have the Royal Receptions continue even after he became too old to host them and said he was passing the title along to his daughter for that reason.[9] The Royal Reception has become a tradition at Nemacolin Woodlands Resort, and so far Joe Hardy shows no sign of slowing down.

Comedienne Joan Rivers, right, served as emcee at the 1995 Royal Reception, when Joe Hardy gave his title, Lord of the Manor of Henley-in-Arden, to his daughter Robin Hardy Freed.

use when you say, 'Maggie.' Empathy. She immediately puts herself in that person's place."[25]

Christina Toras, an attorney and administrative assistant who worked closely with both Joe and Maggie Hardy, agreed.

"I think [Maggie] makes a real effort to get to know who it is that's working for her," Toras said. "She does have one–on–one relationships with the people that work for her, and she is generally a person that cares about her employees and cares about what's going on in their lives and makes you feel very comfortable when you're talking to her."[26]

Dan Hixenbaugh, one of the company's most senior employees, remarked, "Maggie is a fireball. ... [And] she's smart as hell."[27]

A Dedicated Worker

During the time that Maggie Hardy began taking the reins at 84 Lumber, another young woman was drawing Joe Hardy's attention with her hard work and determination.

Deborah Maley had started working at 84 Lumber in 1986, when she was just 15 years old.[28] The job began as a part-time, after-school venture.[29] Debbie Maley had heard favorable reports about the company from her older sister Sherrie, who was a long-time 84 Lumber employee.[30]

Maley took her job very seriously, often punching out on the time clock but continuing to work until 9 or 10 at night.[31]

"There were a lot of different times... when I was in high school, [when kids] were going maybe to a party or I missed things because I had to come to work, but that was OK because I was really having a ball with what I was doing," she said.[32]

It was not long before Maley was promoted from her receptionist position and began to climb the ladder of success at 84 Lumber.[33] Through her various stages of promotion she learned about many different aspects of the company and of the lumber business in general.

Maley recalled that when she was 17 years old, she was promoted to a position in the purchasing department. On her first day in the lumberyard

---

Above: Employees celebrate the opening of the 400th 84 Lumber store in Ephrata, Pennsylvania, at the Elkins Forest Festival Parade. Former Philadelphia Eagles quarterback Ron Jaworski served as celebrity guest at the 1997 opening.

Left: 84 Lumber employees Kurt Stump, left, and Jerry Smith take charge of the grill at a company picnic.

Opposite: Joe Hardy shows his company spirit with an 84 Lumber decal on his new truck.

she came to work wearing high heels, and Gail Baughman, her supervisor at the time, advised her to find some work boots before returning the next day.[34]

Baughman became one of Maley's early mentors at 84 Lumber, and Maley proved that she was a fast learner. By the time she was 19, Maley had become the head of 84 Lumber's customer relations department.[35] She was the first woman to head the department, and most of the people working under her were several years her senior.[36]

Maley was not intimidated, however, and took advantage of every opportunity that 84 Lumber afforded her. Working closely with long-time 84 Lumber associate Denny Brua, she reorganized the customer relations department and made some significant changes.[37]

Maley established 84 Lumber's first toll-free customer service hotline and wrote the first manual to help employees handle customer complaints.[38] She also aggressively pursued vendors to obtain refunds for defective or improperly installed products, saving 84 Lumber a great deal of money and increasing customer satisfaction.[39]

The job required Maley to become familiar with all of 84 Lumber's products and services in order to answer customers' questions, and she dedicated herself to the work.[40]

Debbie Maley's big break came when she met Joe Hardy for the first time. She was delivering a presentation on her department to Hardy and a group of 84 Lumber vice presidents. Maley recalled that she was so nervous about giving the presentation that she could hardly sleep the night before.[41] However, Denny Brua encouraged her and assured her that she was equal to the task, and once Maley was in front of her audience, her natural poise and confidence took over.[42]

She outlined the changes that she had made in the customer relations department and, to Hardy's delight, all the money that she had saved the company.[43] At the end of her presentation, Hardy stood up and applauded and told the executives in attendance that 84 Lumber needed more people like Debbie Maley.[44]

When Maley relayed the comment to Denny Brua later that day, he assured her that if she had won Hardy's approval, she had met the standards of her toughest customer.[45]

After that meeting, Maley said that she often heard reports from other employees that Joe Hardy had mentioned her favorably.[46] She continued to put in long hours and work to make sure that her department was as successful as it could be.

Long Hours, Tough Tests

While Maley was moving quickly through the company's ranks, Maggie Hardy was beginning to take on major responsibilities at 84 Lumber.

When Maggie began a search for a personal assistant, Maley applied for the job.[47] Soon afterward, Maley received word that Joe Hardy wanted to speak to her. She arrived at his office and found him with his feet up on the desk, chewing a cigar.[48]

Hardy told her that, rather than working for Maggie, he wanted her to be his personal assistant, while also helping his daughter.[49] He warned her that the job would involve long hours and a six-day work week, but Maley was unfazed.[50] She remembered:

> I said, "Well, Joe, I don't feel that I'll let you down. I will do a very good job, and I will work really hard. There are a lot of things that I don't know." I said, "If you're willing to keep me, I'm the person to work for you because I'm certainly not afraid of you."[51]

Joe and Debbie Hardy have two daughters together—Paige, front, who was born in 1995, and Taylor, left, born in 1997. The couple determined that, despite the family's wealth, their daughters would be taught the value of hard work.

Once she started her new job, Maley strove to make sure that her duties were not purely secretarial. She continued to work with the customer relations department in addition to organizing Hardy's schedule and making some of the construction arrangements for the recently purchased Nemacolin Woodlands Resort.[52]

Hardy was pleased with her efficiency and began greeting her each morning by saying, "Debbie, Debbie Do, it's Joe, what's new today?" Maley would reply by giving him a rundown of the day's activities, a list which she said always had to include detailed information, and suggested solutions to problems, not just a bare outline of a plan.[53]

Maley recalled that Hardy would regularly test her work ethic and her integrity. One time, she said, he left a large amount of cash in his desk drawer, knowing that Maley would be cleaning the desk.[54] Maley said she recognized immediately that she was being tested and asked her boss to remove the money from the desk and put it in a safer place.[55] It was typical of Hardy's work style to test his business associates at every opportunity in this way.

Maley, however, passed every test with flying colors. After a time Hardy offered her the opportunity to expand her business skills by enrolling in a real estate sales course, for which 84 Lumber would pay.[56] Maley agreed and began going to class after her 12-hour workdays at 84 Lumber.[57]

She earned her real estate license and today owns two real estate businesses.[58] Maley said she appreciated the fact that she had a boss who tried to help her reach her full potential and who took such an interest in all his friends, family members, and employees:

I'm very appreciative because he's given me many opportunities. ... I've been able to help so many people and change their lives because of my affiliation with him. ... I think... that he'll be remembered for... all of the great things that he did for so many other people.[59]

Personal Upheaval

In 1991, Maggie Hardy began dating Peter Magerko, director of security at Nemacolin Woodlands Resort.[60] The two were soon engaged to be married, and Maley, who had become friends with Maggie Hardy, was in charge of arranging the wedding plans.

As Maggie Hardy came closer and closer to her wedding day, her father began to depend increasingly on Maley to accompany him on weekend business trips.

During the same period, Hardy's relationship with Dottie, his wife of nearly 50 years, had begun to deteriorate. Maggie recalled that, while her parents' relationship had had its ups and downs over the years, their expectations about how they would spend their later years drove a wedge between them that led to a divorce.

"At 61, he buys Nemacolin at the point she's thinking in their lives they're going to kind of slow down at least a little bit," Maggie said.[61]

According to long-time family friend Ginny Hackman, Dottie "needed some peace and quiet... a more settled routine. He hadn't changed."[62]

Maley said she never expected her business relationship with Hardy to blossom into a personal one. But when he began calling her at home on the pretext of discussing travel plans, she said, she knew that the nature of their relationship was changing, and the two became romantically involved.

While Joe and Dottie Hardy's breakup was difficult for family and friends to understand, it was even harder for 84 Lumber employees to grasp.

"When this happened, people were confused, very, very confused," Maggie said. "Because they looked at my dad as a rock. ... He never swayed on anything that he ever said was the way it should be. ... They didn't know if 84 would even survive... the financial burden of the divorce."[63]

Hardy and Maley began living together, and Maley made the decision to stop working at 84 Lumber because she did not feel that she could both work and live with Hardy.

However, Hardy claimed that he could never find a better assistant and sometimes asked Maley to come to the office and organize his files for the "generous" salary of $10 an hour. Maley also helped to train new employees at 84 Lumber and generally remained involved with the company.

In 1995, Maley and Hardy's first child, Paige, was born. Maley recalled that she was in labor in the hospital when Hardy told her that he had to go to Nemacolin Woodlands Resort to meet with some politicians.

The doctors told him that it would be impossible for him to drive to the resort and back before the baby was born, so Hardy called a helicopter to take him there.

Once he got there, however, he was so flustered and anxious to go that when the visiting politicians asked him for a $10,000 donation he wrote out a check for $100,000 and made his way back to the helicopter!

He arrived at the hospital before his daughter was born, and Maley recalled that his overjoyed political friends sent a beautiful set of sterling silver baby gifts in appreciation.

Maley and Hardy's second daughter, Taylor, was born in 1997, and Hardy and Maley were married 13 days later.

As Paige and Taylor grew up, Joe and Debbie Hardy determined that, despite the family's wealth, they would make sure that Joe Hardy's two youngest daughters were taught the value of hard work and of earning their way through life. Debbie Hardy explained:

Joe is not a bragging person, you see from his appearance, and... I want to instill in [our children that] they are no better than anyone else, and I want them to work very, very hard because [they] would be very shortchanged if they were to just get everything handed to them. ... They'll work very hard because that's how they will learn how

Maggie Hardy Magerko enjoys an 84 Lumber company picnic with her husband, Peter Magerko, and son, P. J. The husband and wife met at Nemacolin Woodlands Resort, where Peter Magerko worked as director of security.

to run businesses... and be respectful of what their father has accomplished.[64]

Meanwhile, one of Joe Hardy's older daughters was putting that theory into practice. Maggie Hardy's wedding, which featured fireworks and a 10-foot-tall cake, had come off beautifully, and she now went by her married name of Maggie Hardy Magerko.[65]

She had also had a child of her own, Peter Jon Magerko Jr., known as P. J.

Maggie's Building Solutions

Despite these momentous changes in her personal life, Hardy Magerko remained focused on the success of 84 Lumber. After investigating several innovative approaches, she decided to establish a new store that was all her own, one that would explore markets that traditional 84 Lumber stores did not serve.

The result was Maggie's Building Solutions, an upscale building supply and home decorating store. Joe Hardy had experimented with upscale products in the past, with limited success. Now Maggie Hardy Magerko designed a store that could cater both to contractors and to the high-end home-improvement customer.

While 84 Lumber provided homebuilders with all the basic supplies they needed, the new store would offer an array of upscale and custom-designed

products for homeowners and contractors who wanted to create unique homes.

Bob MacKinney and other committed 84 Lumber employees joined in the effort to make Maggie's Building Solutions a success. Gail Baughman had been manager at the lumberyard in Eighty Four,

Opposite top: When the second Maggie's Building Solutions in McMurray, Pennsylvania, opened, managers decided to hire their own team of specially trained installers.

Opposite bottom: Joe Hardy and Maggie Hardy Magerko cut the ribbon at the grand opening of Maggie's Building Solutions. The 7,580-square-foot store included a library where customers could research thousands of home products.

Right: Maggie Hardy Magerko created the new store to reach out to high-end, home-improvement customers, as well as builders interested in designing unique homes.

Below: Functional kitchen appliances added a special touch to displays at Maggie's Building Solutions.

Pennsylvania, for 25 years, but he left that position to take on the new challenge of managing the new store before retiring in 2005 after 38 years with the company.[66]

When it opened in September 1997, the 7,580-square-foot Maggie's Building Solutions store contained a multimedia-equipped conference room and a research library with information about thousands of home products and vendors.[67] The library allowed designers and architects to work with their clients to design dream homes and choose materials.[68]

In addition, Maggie's Building Solutions had its own architectural consultants on staff to help homeowners make decorating decisions.[69] The showroom itself was spectacular. Designed to attract both walk-in customers and large job referrals, the new store featured beautifully designed displays to show off the wide range of home products found at Maggie's.

The new store was not as well suited to contractors as were traditional 84 Lumber outlets because not all materials on display were kept in stock.[70] However, what Maggie's lacked in speed of delivery, it made up for in variety. More than 35 vendors set up displays at Maggie's Building Solutions.[71]

Maggie's Building Solutions was created to provide designer furnishings and fittings for every room in the home. Displays were replaced every few months in order to showcase the wide range of available products, and on-staff architectural consultants used these displays to help customers make decorating decisions for their own homes.

And special touches made the displays even more helpful to buyers. For example, the store's kitchen displays had functional appliances.[72] In order to keep customers coming back and to showcase the full range of designer products available, displays were redesigned or replaced every two to three months.[73]

Although the new store was successful, it became evident after a couple of years that its design and concept needed improvement. These issues were addressed when a second Maggie's Building Solutions was built in McMurray, Pennsylvania.

The new store, which opened in October 1999, cost about $2 million to build,[74] but as Joe Hardy explained to *National Home Center News*, he felt that it was money that needed to be spent if 84 Lumber were to remain competitive in a changing market:

We're dealing with... discriminating customers today, and their house is the reflection of them.

Fifteen years ago, this [showroom] would have been far out, but today it's very contemporary.[75]

One of the most significant improvements at the new store was a change in the way installations were managed. The original Maggie's Building Solutions had been using outside subcontractors to install its fixtures and appliances,[76] but this led to many complaints about improperly installed products.[77]

When the new store was built, the management team at Maggie's got together to address the issue. They decided that the best solution was to hire their own team of installers who would work for the store and be specially trained to install the wide range of products available at the showroom,[78] and a team of 15 installers was brought on staff.[79]

The new store also featured many physical improvements. It was much larger than the previous store, with 17,000 square feet of floor space.[80] The showroom housed 30 kitchen and bath vignette-style displays, each of which was decorated

with details such as groceries, toothbrushes, and soap.[81]

The extra space also allowed the new Maggie's Building Solutions to showcase a wider variety of products. In addition to traditional American brands with which homeowners were familiar, the new store featured many high-quality products from Europe and other parts of the world.[82]

Opposite: Maggie's Building Solutions helped Joe Hardy and Maggie Hardy Magerko achieve their goal of making a connection with upscale customers who wanted more than the basic building supplies available at 84 Lumber.

There was also a playroom, where children could entertain themselves while their parents shopped; a boutique featuring an array of lamps, artwork, and furniture; and a waterfall room.[83]

Both Maggie's Building Solutions locations helped 84 Lumber to achieve the company's goal of making a connection with high-end customers who would not be satisfied with the basic merchandise at a regular 84 Lumber yard.

Now 84 Lumber salespeople could refer customers who wanted more upscale products to the Maggie's stores, and both businesses would profit from the deal. It was all part of the plan that kept 84 Lumber moving forward throughout the 1990s.

Although the past several years had brought the company new heights of prosperity, increased competition from big-box retailers around the turn of the century prompted 84 Lumber to narrow its focus to professional building contractors.

CHAPTER NINE

FINDING NEW DIRECTIONS

The decision was made ... to go after the contractors.... Our mission today is to make the builder the most competitive builder. So we'll do anything that he needs or wants to make him very competitive.

—Joe Hardy, founder of 84 Lumber

ALTHOUGH THE 1990s HAD brought a new level of prosperity and many positive changes to 84 Lumber, not every decision turned out to be good, and thus the company faced several setbacks around the turn of the century.

Especially during the 1980s, Joe Hardy had been so focused on expansion that at times he had overextended the company into markets that could not support new stores. Furthermore, some of the new stores were too small to carry a wide enough range of supplies to compete with other companies,[1] especially "big-box" building supply retailers like The Home Depot and Lowe's. In 2003, Hardy said:

I made a great mistake because I was so interested in expansion. It was like triple-A expansion, but after a while... I wasn't as excited about the operations as I was the expansion. So we probably have closed in the last 15 years, 250 places, because the operations didn't keep up with my... vision of expansion, expansion, expansion, expansion.[2]

Another downside of the massive growth was that it strained the 84 Lumber workforce. The company was committed to its policy of promotion from within, but there were not always enough current employees who were ready to handle managerial responsibilities. When associates with inadequate experience or skills were promoted to management positions, sales faltered and profits dropped.[3]

Competition from larger retailers was another huge challenge. As big-box retailers spread to markets across the country, Hardy considered closing all of his stores and rebuilding the business from scratch, but he decided against that option.[4]

Instead, with his daughter Maggie Hardy Magerko playing a major role in the decision-making process, Hardy resolved to change 84 Lumber's sales focus from targeting do-it-yourself retail customers to professional builders and contractors.

Bill Myrick, who became chief operating officer for 84 Lumber, recalled what became known throughout the company as Hardy's "survival speech," when he outlined the plan for his area managers in November 1991.

He basically said, "If we don't change who our customer is, we're going to go out of business.... We've got to go out, and we've got to go after the contractor...." Here's a guy who had basically done business the same way since 1956, and in [1991],

Joe Hardy and Maggie Hardy Magerko worked to turn the company around after its overexpansion during the 1980s.

he decides he's going to change the customer. Now that was a cultural shock for us.[5]

Once the decision had been made, Joe Hardy and Maggie Hardy Magerko charged ahead with the task of restructuring 84 Lumber to better compete in the new marketplace. Hardy said:

Well, thank God the industry is so large that if you get just a little part of it, you can be highly successful and you get your focus. So the decision was made... to go after the contractors. ... Our mission today is to make the builder the most competitive builder. So we'll do anything that he needs or wants to make him very competitive.[6]

As president of 84 Lumber, Maggie Hardy Magerko led the company's effort to modify the inventory of each store to meet the needs of its area builders.

One of the first and most significant changes was the addition of a professional sales force. Previously, 84 Lumber had relied on its regular associates to make sales, but the company added 450 new sales representatives to help target professional construction customers.[7]

"Contractors are quite a bit more demanding, impatient," said long-time manager Jerry King. "So everybody had to make a lot of adjustment to how to handle the contractors. ... Some of them are more interested in pricing, and some of them are interested in the service. So you've got to be able to do all things for each one of them and find out which one demands the most or what it's going to take to keep that contractor's business."[8]

In addition, the company researched the types of products builders in specific markets were most interested in. Before that time, every 84 Lumber store across the country sold the same mix of products in what Hardy Magerko referred to as a "cookie-cutter" model.[9] Under her direction, the range of products in each store was tailored to meet the specific needs of each region's builders.[10]

"I figured real quick, we need to figure out how to manage 84 on literally a store-by-store basis," Hardy Magerko said.[11]

Even as the company struggled to compete with the big-box retailers, it refused to conform to their way of doing business. Myrick remembered making the decision to offer customers free delivery like The Home Depot and Lowe's did:

Well, Joe got wind that I was going to do this. So, on a Saturday morning, he called me up, and he says, "Hey, Bill, I understand you're going to give free delivery," and I'm like, "Oh, absolutely, Joe, I believe it. This is what Lowe's and Home Depot do, and I think we need to do that to counterbalance it, and I think it will be a good thing."

Then Joe says to me, "Really? ... You have a son, right?" and I said, "Yeah."

"His name is Sean, right?"

I said, "Yeah."

He said, "He's about eight years old, right?"

I said, "Yeah." ...

He said, "Well, one day, Sean is going to be about 16, and... you and your wife may walk into his bedroom and find this leafy stuff in a plastic bag in one of his jacket pockets... called marijuana. You're going to sit down with Sean being the good parent you are, and you're going to say, "Gee, Sean, why do you have this marijuana?" and what he's going to say to you... is, "Dad, everybody else does it."

So needless to say, we did not offer free delivery, and we went out there and continued to charge for delivery, and within three months of us sticking to our policy... Home Depot and Lowe's started charging... because they knew we could.[12]

84 Plus

While the company had begun primarily targeting contractors, 84 Lumber did not give up on retail customers. While some store locations began doing professional builder business exclusively, many more were remodeled to better accommodate the needs of do-it-yourself customers.[13]

Concentrating primarily on stores in rural areas,[14] Hardy Magerko put in motion a plan that would completely change the look of 84 Lumber. The effort to create a balance between retail and professional customers led to the creation of a new type of store called 84 Plus.

At selected 84 Lumber locations, a new section was added with the goal of providing the wide variety of products and services sought by do-it-yourselfers. The typical 20,000-square-foot lumberyards were split into a 10,000-square-foot area that carried basic supplies for contractors and a 10,000-square-foot section for retail shoppers.[15]

In designing 84 Plus, Hardy Magerko and her father disagreed on one key issue. Since the company had been founded, no 84 Lumber store had ever had heating or air conditioning. This cost-cutting measure was known to every 84 Lumber employee as the most famous example of the company's no-frills policy. With the creation of 84 Plus, however, Hardy Magerko argued that to attract more retail customers it was necessary to have a climate-controlled environment.[16] Her father disagreed, but eventually Hardy Magerko won out.

Maggie Hardy Magerko is seen above at an 84 Plus grand opening. Her plan for the new stores included a larger inventory, a racetrack-style layout, and eye-catching displays (bottom). *(Top photo by Michael Redford)*

CHAPEL HONORS HEROES OF FLIGHT 93

JOE HARDY HAD ALWAYS WORKED HARD to see that 84 Lumber stores supported the communities where they were located, and when the terrorist attacks of September 11, 2001, occurred, the events struck close to home for 84 Lumber.

Shanksville, Pennsylvania, where American Airlines Flight 93 crashed into a field after passengers tried to wrest control of the plane from its hijackers, was only about 80 miles away from Eighty Four, Pennsylvania.

After the tragedy, a Shanksville area priest, Reverend Alphonse T. Mascherino, wanted to see a memorial commemorating the heroes of Flight 93 and the other innocent people killed that day. When he learned that it would be 10 to 20 years before an official federal monument could be erected, Mascherino decided to create his own.[1]

He found a 100-year-old church three miles from the crash site that was badly in need of repairs.[2] By selling some of his own belongings, he raised enough money to purchase the church.[3] He then began the huge task of refurbishing the building, asking local vendors for supplies to redecorate the inside.[4] Gradually, during June and July of 2002, people began to hear about the project and volunteer their weekends to help with the reconstruction.[5]

One of these people was Mark Summers, manager of the 84 Lumber store in Somerset, Pennsylvania, 10 miles away from the church.[6] After visiting the property, Summers realized that Mascherino would need thousands of dollars' worth of supplies and many hours of labor to complete the project. Summers drew up a list of needed supplies and called Maggie Hardy Magerko to ask her if 84 Lumber would be willing to make a contribution to the chapel.

Hardy Magerko authorized the costs and told Summers that 84 Lumber would provide whatever supplies were needed to finish the church,[7] a total of $23,117 worth of materials.[8]

The only challenge remaining was that Hardy Magerko thought the church should be completed in time for the one-year anniversary of the tragedy, which was less than two weeks away. Emulating her father's "nothing is impossible"

This was only one of the changes that made 84 Plus stores more attractive to shoppers. The new stores carried about 12,000 products as opposed to the 3,000 or 4,000 found at a typical 84 Lumber store.[17] Furthermore, the new store had a racetrack-style layout and featured special displays to capture customers' attention.[18]

After trying out the concept with a test store in Winchester, Tennessee, 84 Lumber opened its first 84 Plus stores in Graysville, Tennessee, and Findley, Ohio, in April 1999.[19] The Graysville store featured a Home Décor department,[20] as well as paint-mixing and seasonal departments.[21]

Although the greater product diversity and more comfortable environment would increase costs,

Hardy Magerko believed that 84 Plus stores would help to increase the company's profits by selling products at a higher profit margin.[22]

84 Plus outlets were soon opening at 84 Lumber locations in various states across the country, and in the new millennium, 84 Plus continued to expand as part of Hardy Magerko's plan to keep the stores competitive.

The company identified 1,000 potential markets for 84 Plus stores, most of them in rural areas where competition was at a minimum.[23] Once an 84 Lumber store was chosen as a new 84 Plus location, it took only about a month to remodel the warehouse.[24] In the early years of the 21st century, more than a hundred 84 Plus stores would open.[25]

attitude, Hardy Magerko authorized Summers to hire as many contractors as he would need to finish the building in time for a memorial service on September 11, 2002.[9]

Once he was given the go-ahead, Summers sprang into action. 84 Lumber volunteers and contractors worked day and night to insulate, drywall, and paint the chapel. Other area vendors also donated their time and supplies to help make the building beautiful. The crowning touch to the church was a large steel bell tower, donated by 84 Lumber, that was preconstructed and lifted by a crane into its place at the church entrance.[10] The tower was topped with an antique bell that Mascherino named "Thunder Bell: The Voice of Flight 93."[11]

Thanks to the generosity and dedication of 84 Lumber and other merchants and volunteers, the chapel was completed in time for the anniversary, and on the afternoon of September 11, 2002, a crowd gathered for a memorial service to honor the fallen heroes.[12]

84 Lumber associates worked around the clock to spruce up this Pennsylvania church in time for the one-year anniversary of the September 11, 2001, attacks. The memorial chapel's crowning touch was an antique bell donated by 84 Lumber that was christened "Thunder Bell: The Voice of Flight 93."

A dedication ceremony was held at the chapel, with a special tribute to firefighters and service personnel,[13] and 84 Lumber associates who worked on the project said they were proud of their efforts to help honor those who had died.

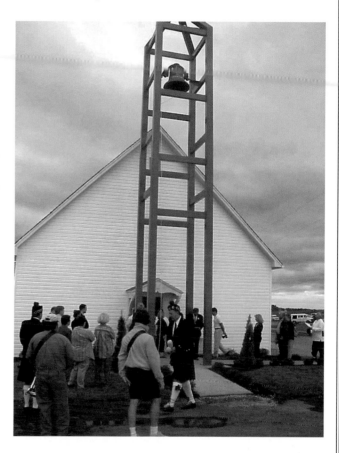

Moving West

At the same time, a new, reconsidered expansion plan was put into place with the primary goal of increasing 84 Lumber's presence in the western United States. Although the company already had some stores in the region, it had many more clustered closer to its home base in Pennsylvania. 84 Lumber was able to expand significantly in the West by buying a number of stores from Payless-Cashways, a building products competitor that had stores in many western U.S. markets that 84 Lumber had not yet penetrated.

According to Hardy Magerko, Payless-Cashways had also been hurt by the spread of big-box retailers, but because it was a publicly traded company, it was unable to shift its focus to contractors as quickly as 84 Lumber had.[26]

When dozens of Payless-Cashways stores went up for auction in a bankruptcy sale, Joe Hardy flew to all the potential properties, picked the locations he liked best, and bought them.[27] This move helped 84 Lumber break into new markets, such as the Las Vegas area, one of the largest housing markets in the country during the early 2000s.[28]

The Payless-Cashways stores were quickly refurbished and scheduled to be reopened in a matter of months. As a result, Maggie Hardy Magerko and Joe Hardy soon found themselves with 20 stores scheduled to open in one day, the greatest number of simultaneous grand openings in the company's history.

The openings included 18 former Payless-Cashways facilities, as well as two new locations in Bessemer, Alabama, and Fruitland, Maryland.[29] This increased the size of the chain by nearly 5 percent, to 434 stores in 34 states.[30] The move took 84 Lumber into three new states—Nebraska, Nevada, and Oklahoma—and increased its presence in other growing markets.[31]

In the meantime, the company had to find enough qualified managers to staff the new stores,[32] an issue that had plagued 84 Lumber during its rapid expansion in the past.

At first, Frank Cicero, 84 Lumber's vice president of operations, was reluctant to bring the Payless-Cashways managers on board, and Hardy Magerko feared they might not be able to finalize the acquisition without qualified staff to operate the new stores. She remembered that it was her father, Joe Hardy, who persuaded her to move ahead with the deal.

Hardy Magerko recalled her father telling her, "You've got to do this. [You've] got to take a risk in life."[33] In the end, Hardy Magerko made the decision to retain Payless-Cashways managers at 15 of the stores.[34]

"We were very fortunate that many of the former Payless-Cashways managers were highly experienced in both the industry and their local market," Cicero said. "The experience and local market knowledge and contacts of the managers also played a critical role in our ability to quickly recruit and train experienced contractor sales representatives."[35]

When the day of the grand openings arrived, Maggie Hardy Magerko and Joe Hardy set out on a grueling schedule to attend all 20 in one day. This was a tall order because the new stores stretched from California to Delaware.[36]

However, Hardy had personally attended every grand opening to date and was not about to break his record. Taking advantage of time zone changes and flying in Hardy's private jet, the two managed to make an appearance at all 20 grand openings within a day and a half.[37]

As months passed, it became more and more apparent that the new focus on contractors was yielding positive results. The newly hired sales force accounted for as much as 85 percent of sales at each store.[38] Professional builders tended to provide more repeat business than do-it-yourselfers, a strong advantage enhanced by the fact that the pro market was larger than the amateur home improvement market.[39]

At first, Hardy Magerko said, some of the company's long-time managers had trouble making the shift to contractor sales:

Managing a store that way is a lot more complicated because you have to understand each phase of each of your contractors' business[es], and you have to anticipate your inventory a lot different[ly] than... when you had it on the shelf, and it was just an automatic replenishment system. The ironic thing is, our best salesmen today are some of those managers [who]... said they couldn't do it. However, today they're outside salesmen doing millions of dollars.[40]

In the interest of attracting even more professional builders, 84 Lumber, built on the principle of cash and carry, began to grant greater amounts of credit than ever before. By 2002, 80 percent of the company's sales were done on an accounts receivable basis,[41] and sales at stores that had been open more than a year rose by 25 percent.[42]

84 Lumber also began opening more component manufacturing plants that assembled building materials such as panels and trusses in order to reduce costs on these essential items even further for professional customers.[43]

All of these victories came together to help 84 Lumber reach an important milestone. On December 7, 2002, the company exceeded $2 billion in annual sales for the first time in its history.[44] This represented a 16.5 percent increase above the previous year's sales.[45]

Maggie Hardy Magerko remarked, "The success would not have been possible without each and every one of our associates."[46]

Family Loses Its Rock

For the Hardy family, however, the news was tempered by the death of Dottie Hardy after a difficult battle with lung cancer just a few days earlier, on December 3, 2002. Those who knew her talked about the extraordinary life she had led.

Susan Gillespie, Ed and Ann Ryan's daughter, told the *Pittsburgh Post-Gazette*, "She could wear diamonds, but she also could wear blue jeans. She didn't put on airs. She always was in a good mood and was very good about rolling with the punches. I can't in a lifetime think of one bad thing about her."[47]

Hardy Magerko said, "If you talk to anyone and you ask what they'd say about my mom, they'd say she's the... classiest person they've ever met."[48]

According to daughter Robin Hardy Freed, her parents made peace toward the end of Dottie's life, "My father was wonderful with my mother at the end, just wonderful," she said. "He gave her a great deal of comfort during [her] last month... as he did his children."[49]

World-Class Resort, Hardy-Style

In the meantime, Joe Hardy's new project, the Nemacolin Woodlands Resort, was blossoming. After he purchased the property in 1987, Hardy had poured his money and energy into improving it. His first move

Above: Dorothy "Dottie" Pierce Hardy, seen here as a young woman, died on December 3, 2002, of lung cancer. She was 79. Family, friends, and acquaintances described her as classy, gracious, and down-to-earth. She was survived by her five children—Joseph, Paul, Robin, Kathy, and Maggie—as well as 13 grandchildren and two great-grandchildren.

Right: Joe and Dottie Hardy were married for 54 years before they divorced in 1997. Family members said that Joe and Dottie made peace with each other toward the end of Dottie's life. *(Photo by Michael Redford)*

had been to renovate and expand the Tudor-style lodge that was already on the property when he purchased it, and to build the Woodlands Spa.[50]

Several other important developments at Nemacolin Woodlands Resort had taken place during the 1990s. In 1992, an equestrian center was added to the resort,[51] and during the same year, ground was broken for a second golf course.[52]

While the resort already had one golf course, The Links,[53] Hardy had bigger dreams. He hired legendary golf course designer Pete Dye to create a world-class course for the Nemacolin Woodlands Resort.[54] The result was Mystic Rock, an 18-hole course that offered breathtaking views of the wooded hills surrounding the property.

Don Gearhart, whose company did most of the earth-moving work for the golf course, recalled that Joe Hardy was a strict taskmaster, demanding quick results and unsurpassed quality on all Nemacolin Woodlands Resort projects, just as he did at 84 Lumber.

[Joe Hardy] was 15 percent of our sales over the years. It took 98 percent of our effort. … [He's] very

Opposite: Joe Hardy emulated the Paris Ritz hotel with the $65 million Chateau LaFayette, which was completed in 1997.

Above: Botero's Fat Bird, featured in Nemacolin's logo, is just one of several pieces of art dotting the resort's landscape.

Below: Designed by Maggie Hardy Magerko, the resort's world-class Woodlands Spa was among the first projects at Nemacolin. It opened in 1988. *(Photos courtesy of Nemacolin Woodlands Resort and Spa)*

Traditional leisure activities at the resort include tennis and golf, as well as horseback riding, miniature golf, shopping, and fine dining. *(Photos courtesy of Nemacolin Woodlands Resort and Spa)*

demanding. … He doesn't want to have a supervisor over you. He wants you to supervise. Expects an awful lot out of you. … When he gets an idea, he wants it and he wants it now, and he wants it right.[55]

The work by Gearhart and other contributors to Mystic Rock paid off. The course was unveiled in September 1995 in conjunction with the first Mystic Rock Challenge.[56] Champion golfer Tiger Woods, fresh from winning the Masters, played in the tournament[57] and was only the first in a string of famous golfers who would play the course.

Other important additions to Nemacolin Woodlands Resort included the Paradise Pool, a tropical pool featuring a swim-up bar, and the Mystic Mountain ski resort, offering a variety of winter activities.[58] For the relaxed visitor, a shopping arcade was added, while an activities course—including a climbing wall, in-line skating, and a ropes course—provided entertainment for the more adventurous.[59]

According to Jeff Kmiec, vice president of marketing for 84 Lumber, "Mr. Hardy's desire, and Maggie's, has always been to keep the resort as contemporary as possible. So they always add the newest and the most interesting… activities or amenities… to make sure the resort is… never stagnant or stale and… always at the cutting edge of the resort industry."[60]

In addition, Joe Hardy had decided that the 98-room English Tudor-style lodge that he had renovated when he first purchased the Nemacolin property was no longer sufficient to meet the needs of the growing resort. While on a trip to Paris he was smitten by the graceful elegance of the Ritz hotel, and upon returning to the United States, Hardy determined to recreate the hotel at Nemacolin Woodlands Resort.[61]

Maggie Hardy Magerko's husband, Pete, who worked with Joe Hardy on construction and development at the resort, said, "He wasn't even back

from his trip yet, and he had an architect flying over there from Pittsburgh with a camera."[62]

Hardy hired a team of American designers and launched into a $65 million dollar project to recreate the Ritz, down to the Palladian windows and coffered ceilings of the European original.[63] In some ways, Hardy's new hotel, named the Chateau LaFayette, was even more luxurious than the original. For example, its guest rooms boasted 14-foot ceilings, higher than those at the Ritz.[64]

Nemacolin continued to add amenities for every type of guest, including the Mystic Mountain ski resort, top left, and an activities course with a climbing wall, top right, in-line skating, and a ropes course. Less adventurous visitors can spend time biking around the property, right, or relaxing in the Paradise Pool, below, a tropical-themed pool area that featured a swim-up bar. *(Photos courtesy of Nemacolin Woodlands Resort and Spa)*

Inside, the Chateau LaFayette offered 124 beautifully appointed guest rooms, the most luxurious a 1,600-square-foot penthouse on the fifth floor, with its own private roof garden, two bedrooms, and a living and dining area.[65] The Chateau LaFayette was completed in 1997.[66]

'Obstacles Are Opportunities'

During the ongoing construction, the resort's hospitality staff found innovative ways of keeping things running smoothly for the guests. Wanda Anker, director of recruiting, recalled a blizzard during the winter of 1993 that proved the resort's employees were up for the challenge of working for Joe Hardy.

We had a blizzard here that... dumped 42 inches of snow in a matter of hours... to the point where we were snowed in... and we used horses to get around... the property. ... It actually was fun figuring out our challenges. All of us that had four-wheel drives were picking up our hourly staff so that we could service our guests. [We didn't have] power, [but] it didn't matter.[67]

Anker said typical winter weather didn't slow progress on Chateau LaFayette, either. In order to continue construction during winter months, workers constructed a plastic dome to cover the site.

"What we've learned is [that] obstacles are opportunities," she said. "They give you an opportunity to step outside the box and say, 'OK, how can we do this a different way?' "[68]

Trey Matheu, director of resort operations, said, "We can get away with doing some neat stuff and some off-the-wall thinking. Sometimes we fall flat on our faces, but more often than not, these are the ideas that really push it out there."

Matheu remembered that one Monday, three Hummer military vehicles were delivered to the resort, and Hardy called soon after to ask Tom Smith, the

In some ways, Nemacolin's Chateau LaFayette, featuring 124 guest rooms, is even more luxurious than its inspiration, the Ritz hotel in Paris. *(Photo courtesy of Nemacolin Woodlands Resort and Spa)*

resort's director of recreation and activities, if he could create a Hummer obstacle course by Saturday.

"To Tom's [credit], he jumped right on it," Matheu said. "[He] got a Bobcat out there, cut down some trees. created some activities and some obstacles, and had it up and running for our first paying people five days later."[69]

In the new millennium, Hardy continued his campaign to transform Nemacolin Woodlands Resort into one of the country's premiere resorts. In 2002, a new amenity, Woodlands World, was opened.[70] The 50,000-square-foot complex offered a variety of outdoor shops[71] and included a gun museum with a collection of more than 460 early American firearms.[72] The following year,

Golfers who participated in the first 84 Lumber Classic tournament in 2003 had plenty of compliments for the accommodations, food, and amenities at Nemacolin Woodlands Resort. *(Photo courtesy of Nemacolin Woodlands Resort and Spa)*

the John Daly Golf Learning Center opened at the Mystic Rock golf course[73] featuring an indoor classroom with putting greens, as well as video equipment.[74]

As part of a $20 million renovation to turn Mystic Rock into a PGA Tour-level course, Hardy added a $600,000 waterfall to help enhance the golf course's beauty.

Word Gets Out

The growing reputation of Mystic Rock was one of the crowning achievements in Joe Hardy's and Maggie Hardy Magerko's renovation of the resort. Joe Hardy had built Mystic Rock at Nemacolin Woodlands Resort because he felt that a world-class resort needed a world-class golf course. But for the course to be truly appreciated, it needed to host some of golf's greatest competitors.

This dream came to fruition in 2003 when Mystic Rock hosted the 84 Lumber Classic, part of the Professional Golf Association's annual tour.[75] Previously called the Pennsylvania Classic, the competition had a purse of $4 million and brought golfers from around the world to the resort and the improved Mystic Rock course.[76]

Securing the right to host the tournament was no easy task. When PGA official John Mutch first visited the site in 2002, he noted several changes that needed to be made in order to turn Mystic Rock into a PGA Tour–level course.[77] Mutch gave Hardy a list of recommended changes,[78] and Hardy, true to form, went above and beyond what was asked of him, spending $20 million on course renovations.[79] Thousands of tons of white sand were hauled in to rebuild the bunkers, a new $600,000 waterfall was added to enhance the scenic beauty of the course,[80] and the greens were also improved.[81]

None of this attention to detail was lost on the golfers who arrived for the 84 Lumber Classic in September 2003. A week of festivities at Nemacolin

Joe Hardy greets President Bill Clinton during a visit to Nemacolin Woodlands Resort in 2000.

Woodlands Resort started off with 96 amateur golfers competing in the Mystic Pro-Am,[82] but the event was cut short by heavy rain.[83] Weather troubles continued to plague the 84 Lumber Classic that year, but many of the participants found that their disappointment with the soggy golfing conditions was tempered by the fun they were having at the resort.

Hardy had pulled out all the stops to welcome the pro golfers, and scheduled events included a Bass Classic fishing competition for PGA players, their families, and friends,[84] as well as dinners with Joe Hardy and Maggie Hardy Magerko. As the tournament progressed, many of the golfers complimented both the Mystic Rock course and Nemacolin Woodlands Resort.

Dennis Paulson, one of the participating golfers, told reporters from the Uniontown *Herald-Standard*, "If a storm is going to hit, this is the place to be. … I took my kid fishing yesterday for an hour-and-a-half. Then we played some miniature golf. All the rooms are first-rate. The whole place is just phenomenal."[85]

Rocco Mediate, who finished fifth in the tournament, agreed, "Joe put on a good show. Everything was great here... the course, the resort. The players were treated well. The food was great, probably the best on [the] tour. … I think guys will continue to flock back here, and once the word gets out, once guys start telling everyone what a great experience they had, then it can only become more popular."[86]

When the tournament concluded on September 21, golfer J. L. Lewis walked away with a total score of 266 over four rounds[87] and the $720,000 first prize.[88] The next year, Vijay Singh, ranked the No. 1 golfer in the world in 2004, garnered the top honor with a score of 273. But Joe Hardy and

Maggie Hardy Magerko felt like the real winners. The tournament had garnered coverage on ESPN, displaying the beauty of Mystic Rock and Nemacolin Woodlands Resort to television viewers across the country. Furthermore, Mystic Rock was scheduled to continue hosting the tour until at least 2006.

Joe Hardy and Maggie Hardy Magerko's involvement in the PGA Tour led to 84 Lumber's sponsorships of professional golfers John Daly and Singh. According to Jeff Kmiec, vice president of marketing, Daly is an ideal representative for 84 Lumber

because blue-collar males identify so strongly with him. In addition, events such as the company's John Daly Invitational and other personal appearances

President George W. Bush poses for a photo with the Hardy family during his visit to Nemacolin Woodlands Resort in 2001. In the back row, from left to right, are Robin Freed, Kathy Drake, President Bush, Joe Hardy, and Maggie Hardy Magerko. In the front row are Paige Hardy, left, and Taylor Hardy.

by Daly at contractor events, allow professional builders a "once-in-a-lifetime opportunity to get close to a PGA pro," and help 84 Lumber develop long-term relationships with target customers.

The company began its relationship with Singh when the golfer visited Mystic Rock to practice playing the course before the 84 Lumber Classic. Hardy was so impressed with Singh's work ethic and desire to play the best game possible that he decided to sponsor the golfer.[89]

As usual, Hardy refused to rest on his laurels. No sooner had the first tournament concluded than

Right: 84 Lumber's sponsorship of golfer John Daly has helped the company foster relationships with professional builders.

Below: The 84 Lumber Classic has become Nemacolin Woodlands Resort's flagship event. More than 150,000 people attended the 2004 tournament at the resort, one of the premiere stops on the PGA Tour. (Photos courtesy of Crystal Images/84 Lumber Classic)

With a total score of 273, Vijay Singh, ranked the No. 1 golfer in the world in 2004, won the 84 Lumber Classic that year. A day before the tournament began, 84 Lumber had announced it would sponsor Singh. *(Photo courtesy of Crystal Images/84 Lumber Classic)*

he was back to the drawing board, dreaming up new ways to improve the resort.

Jerry Maley, Debbie Hardy's father, remarked, "[Joe] always made the statement [that] the only thing they didn't have up there [at Nemacolin Woodlands Resort] was the ocean, and he's working on that, and I'm not even wanting to think about that. He's liable to try."[90]

Despite the extensive changes at the resort, associates marveled at the fact that Hardy's vision for it had remained constant.

According to Anker, "The mission statement talks about, first of all, our goal of being a luxurious resort dedicated to providing the highest standard of friendly service... and luxurious accommodations. That was written back in 1987 when we only had 30 rooms in the original section. [The mission] has not changed."[91]

What's in a Name?

Jobs
Optimistic
Enthusiastic
Honest
American
Republican
Determined
Your Commissioner

Paid for by friends of Joe Hardy

At 80 years old, Joe Hardy turned his ambitions to politics, running for commissioner in Fayette County, Pennsylvania, where Nemacolin Woodlands Resort is located. His goal was to transform the area into a place that would attract younger people.

CHAPTER TEN

LOOKING AHEAD

Anyplace I go, it's not to enjoy myself. My enjoyment is to see if I can't steal an idea. ... Learn, learn, learn. You keep learning. That makes it fun.

—Joe Hardy, founder of 84 Lumber

JOE HARDY REACHED AN IMPORtant milestone on January 7, 2003, when he celebrated his 80th birthday. He marked the occasion by spending the day with two of his daughters, Maggie Hardy Magerko and Robin Hardy Freed.

The three flew to Florida to witness Jeb Bush's gubernatorial inauguration and then celebrated with a birthday luncheon.[1] The day ended with dinner in New Orleans and a flight back to Florida,[2] where the trio spent the night at Hardy Magerko's Boca Raton condominium and watched the sunrise the next morning.[3]

For Hardy, becoming an octogenarian was no excuse to slow down, and shortly after his birthday he embarked on an entirely new challenge—politics—and the upcoming county commission race in Fayette County, where the Nemacolin Woodlands Resort is located.

Fayette County was an economically troubled area. At one time, the county had been home to millionaires, many of whom made their fortunes from mining a large coal bed in the area.[4] When the coal ran out, however, so did Fayette's fortunes. In the 1950s, the coal mining industry declined, eliminating thousands of jobs and raising unemployment rates as high as 25 percent.[5] As the decades passed, Fayette County continued to struggle with unemployment and an increasing welfare roll.[6]

By the time Hardy decided to run for office, Fayette County was still one of the poorest counties in the state.[7] But Hardy saw the difficulties as an opportunity, a chance to give something back to the community and to expand his own horizons.

Hardy decided to run as a Republican, a risky choice in Fayette County, where registered Democrats outnumbered Republicans three to one.[8] In March 2003, Hardy approached the county's GOP chairman about his candidacy. Some of the other candidates found it hard to believe that Hardy was sincere in his desire to run for office.

Sean Cavanagh, a Democrat and a Fayette County commissioner at the time, joked, "Maybe [Hardy's] doing it for the money."[9] The job paid only about $40,000 a year, compared to the millions generated by 84 Lumber and Nemacolin Woodlands.

Other candidates, although they admitted that Hardy's business expertise could be an asset to the commission if he were elected, wondered why Hardy had chosen to enter the race and whether he would be able to tolerate the constant public scrutiny that comes with political office.[10] Many

Joe Hardy viewed involvement in politics as a way to give back to a struggling community.

residents of the area were unsure whether Hardy's plan to run for office was a joke.[11]

But Hardy showed them that he wasn't kidding. His own explanation for running for office was simple. He said, "It sounds corny, but [I've] been very successful in many, many things, and it's sort of time I... give back at 80 years old."[12]

In response to the area's economic and employment issues, Hardy's platform was also simple: "Jobs, jobs, jobs!" Calling on some of the friends he had made during his years in the lumber business, Hardy began campaigning for the office. He approached the task with the same improvisational tactics that he used in running his business.

Bink Conover, one of Hardy's oldest friends, recalled Hardy's fundraising dinner. He said Hardy seldom had a speech prepared for any occasion, and as the time for Hardy to speak to his potential donors arrived, Conover asked Hardy what he planned to say when he took the stage.[13] Hardy replied, "I don't know, but I will when I get up there."[14]

Campaign advertisements during Joe Hardy's run for Fayette County commissioner emphasized his commitment to creating jobs. His desire to work with members of both political parties helped him win a seat on the commission, even though he ran as a Republican in the Democrat-leaning region.

This mailer promoted the Mystic Rock golf course and clubhouse at Nemacolin Woodlands Resort, as well as Hardy's bid for office.

A Political Upset

In the May 2003 Republican primary, Hardy was the top vote-getter of six candidates.[15] He and second-place runner Angela Zimmerlink received the party's nomination for county commissioner, and the next leg of the race was on.[16]

Hardy appealed to voters with the promise that he was willing to do whatever was necessary to attract new business to Fayette County. He pledged to use his private jet to travel across the United States to investigate growing businesses, and to bring his fellow commissioners with him, all at his own expense.[17] His plan was to utilize tax concessions and the "red carpet treatment" to entice expanding companies to set up branches in Fayette County, thereby creating jobs and fueling the economy.[18]

Hardy also proposed plans to renovate the county courthouse and build a new airport in the area.[19] Perhaps most importantly, he expressed a desire to work with both Democrats and Republicans, and anyone else, to get the job done.[20] His no-nonsense approach and disdain for political red tape appealed to many voters, who had grown tired of political infighting that seemed to hamper progress. Hardy hoped to use in politics the same aggressive, no-holds-barred approach that had served him so well in building 84 Lumber.

Jerry Maley, Debbie Hardy's father, recalled, "[Hardy] told me, 'I'm tired of that county being so run down. I want to build that county up.' I don't know what else you would want out of a commissioner."[21]

Voters agreed. By the time election day arrived on November 4, 2003, four candidates were still competing for Fayette County's three commissioner positions. Incumbent Vincent Vicites and challenger J. William Lincoln ran on the Democratic ticket, and Hardy and Zimmerlink represented the Republican party.[22] It proved to be a close race.

With 103 of 105 precincts reporting when the story ran in the local *Uniontown Herald-Standard*, only about 3,000 votes separated the first– and fourth–place finishers.[23] Vicites took an early lead, but as more votes were counted Hardy began to gather percentage points.[24] In the end, the winners were Vicites, Hardy, and Zimmerlink, with Hardy running a close second to Vicites for number of votes received.[25] According to an article that appeared the next day in the Pittsburgh *Post-Gazette*:

Hardy began dancing at the Uniontown VFW when it became clear he was elected. "I had a feeling it was going to be really, really close," he said. "I'll try moving up the county from the 64th lousiest county to something better. There will be no committee meetings where we talk, talk, talk. I want to get things done."[26]

The race was an upset. Hardy had used his common man appeal to win over many Democratic voters and had managed to give the Democratic incumbent a run for his money, despite the fact that Hardy had no prior political experience. Furthermore, with both Zimmerlink and Hardy elected, the Fayette County board of commissioners had its first-ever Republican majority.[27]

Almost right away, Hardy began flying around the country to get ideas on how to revitalize the area.

He said, "I go to different towns and see how they've restored [them]… and I asked them one time, 'How long did this take you to accomplish?' They said, 'Oh, between 10 and 12 years.' Well, I want to do that in that many months."[28]

Hardy, who made arrangements to donate his salary to the Fayette County Community Action Food Bank, then launched into what he called the

"Marshall Plan II," with its first phase being the beautification of downtown areas and the second phase bringing in retailers to encourage commerce. In 2004, Hardy told *Mount Lebanon* magazine that his goal in launching a revitalization of the area was to transform Fayette County into a place that will attract young people—and make them want to stay.

"I told the kids that I would like to create things here so they can stay here," he said. "My goal is to stimulate the economy and have things happen."[29]

Breathing Life into Uniontown

Months before securing his spot on the Fayette County Commission, Hardy had already begun mapping out a plan to renovate and revitalize Uniontown, a city of approximately 13,000 residents located about nine miles from Nemacolin Woodlands Resort. Like much of western Pennsylvania, Uniontown had seen its share of prosperity during the coal boom, but during the second half of the 20th century, it fell into an economic slump and never fully recovered.[30]

Further compounding the problem, Uniontown's downtown merchants were hit hard as sprawling shopping malls and large retailers sprang up in surrounding areas, taking shoppers with them. As did many other city centers across the country, downtown Uniontown fell into disrepair, and business owners who expressed interest in moving there were discouraged by the unsightly properties.

"Our downtown had a lot of empty storefronts and vacant buildings, and they were blighted," said

Charmaine Sampson, who worked as administrative assistant to Hardy in his role as commissioner. "They needed to be painted. They needed to be repaired. When you brought somebody into town, they didn't want to look at a building that was in that condition. … [Hardy] ran with the philosophy that we can make it better, and people were ready for a change. They were tired of the fighting, the backbiting, the slander" among local politicians.[31]

While Hardy campaigned hard for his commission seat, he was also busy behind the scenes, working with downtown business owners to find out what the area needed to attract more commerce. Steve Neubauer, a third-generation florist and owner of Neubauer's Flowers, Inc. in downtown Uniontown, had been providing floral arrangements for Nemacolin Woodlands Resort for several years and was impressed by Hardy's ability to get things done.

He remembered Hardy approaching him early on in the campaign with some ideas: "He said, 'If I get elected, I'm going to clean up downtown Union-

town,' and I said, 'That's great. If you need any help, call me.' "

Struck by Hardy's resolve, Neubauer, a lifelong Democrat, said he changed his voter registration so he could support Hardy in the primary, as well as in the general election. Just a few weeks after Hardy took office, he and Neubauer took a Saturday morning drive around Uniontown, and the men brainstormed about the physical improvements that needed to be made.

Neubauer recalled, "After we were done, [Hardy] said, 'How would you like to spend a million dollars?' " Neubauer agreed to help, and he and Hardy began assembling a team to execute the first stage of the plan. From the beginning, Neubauer said, "We were encouraged to not worry about making mistakes because there wasn't anything that we could do that couldn't be fixed. So we aggressively went after it."[32]

As shown above, most of downtown Uniontown was in need of a facelift before the revitalization project began. The renderings below illustrate planned improvements, including new coats of paint, awnings, lamp posts, sidewalk repairs, and greenery.

Above left and at right: Local officials and business owners wanted to ensure the renovations helped enhance the historic look of the city's buildings. (Photos © Tony Marshall)

Hardy established a company, Commercial Center Associates, LLC, to handle the improvements and pledged $1 million of his own money to the streetscaping project, which included painting storefronts, repairing damaged sidewalks, and adding lamp posts, among other improvements. Hardy provided matching funds for business owners who wanted to spruce up their properties, and the city offered no-interest loans to help with the balance. Of the 59 businesses targeted for the first stage of the plan, 57 elected to participate, and Hardy ended up contributing $4 million of his personal funds.[33]

As usual, Hardy planned a nearly unimaginable schedule for completion of the improvements. Bob Junk, president of Commercial Center Associates, said, "People traditionally working in the field of revitalizing a town… take years," but Hardy "stepped up and said, 'Hey, we're going to get it done, and we're going to get it done in 90 days.' … Basically

every piece of property was either touched by a paintbrush or somebody pulling out weeds, mowing the grass, planting flowers, or painting the building, or fixing up the front of that building."[34]

But even more important than the physical improvements was the boost in community pride Hardy inspired.

"The most impressive thing with me is just the enthusiasm and the positive attitude that Joe Hardy brings with him," Neubauer said. "Obviously, the physical things are nice, and they're attractive, but just changing the attitude of the local residents is [the most important]. Getting them to believe in themselves and getting them to feel good about their home again is probably as important to me as a new facade, new sidewalks, and everything else."[35]

To encourage Uniontown residents to come back downtown, the redevelopment team planned and executed several successful events in 2004, including a downtown art festival, an Italian festival, as well as a nostalgic return to a regular farmers' market. At least one festival a month was

More photos above and below show Main Street before and after the physical improvements.

At left and above right: The revitalization project was designed to welcome back people who had become accustomed to shopping at malls and large retailers on the outskirts of town. (Photos © Tony Marshall)

planned for 2005. In addition, the team negotiated with several businesses looking to set up shop in downtown Uniontown.

"We want to be a town. We want to do more things," Junk said. "We're getting people to want to participate in events and participate in [changing] downtown Uniontown. ... It's all fellowship... where people talk and associate with each other and enjoy seeing each other. That's part of... rebuilding downtown Uniontown, getting those people back."[36]

Already, business owners including Neubauer said they were seeing increased foot traffic through the downtown area, as well as more customers in their stores.[37]

Leaders in surrounding communities believed the redevelopment of Uniontown would also benefit their areas. Norma Ryan, mayor of nearby Brownsville, Pennsylvania, said she looked forward to learning from how much Hardy had accomplished in such a short time. "He has a tremendously bright, brilliant business mind," she said.[38]

County Solicitor Joe Ferens added, "I have so much respect for this guy and what he's been able to do and his... catch phrase, 'nothing is impossible.' ... I had about had it with local government and just business in general, and to see a guy like Joe with his wherewithal take on a challenge like this, it kind of enthuses and revitalizes everyone."[39]

While the effort to transform Uniontown into a destination—especially for people accustomed to doing all their shopping at malls—was far from over, many agreed with former state Senator Bill

Lincoln's view that, "if anybody has a chance of successfully bringing that back, it will be him."[40]

"He's a man of action," said fellow Fayette County Commissioner Vince Vicites. "Fayette County is moving forward."[41]

Giving Back

Working as county commissioner was not the only way in which Hardy showed support for the communities and institutions that had served him well over the years. He also made numerous donations to charitable organizations in the interest of putting the wealth generated by 84 Lumber and Nemacolin to good use.

Some of these projects were longstanding. For example, Hardy donated the proceeds from the annual Joe Hardy/84 Lumber Golf Invitational held at Nemacolin Woodlands to the Westmoreland/

Fayette Boy Scout Council.[42] The money was not just a token donation. By 2003 the program had been in place for 14 years, and the organization had received a total of $745,000.[43] The money helped to fund projects such as camping scholarships for children from low-income families and a new "special needs" troop for disabled children.[44]

Another ongoing charitable project was the company's affiliation with Habitat for Humanity. The charity, which builds and renovates homes for disadvantaged families, was a natural partner organization for 84 Lumber, and the company contributed to hundreds of Habitat home projects.

One of the causes that was most important to Hardy was funding scholarships for the families of 84 Lumber employees. The George T. Handyside Memorial Scholarship, which gave assistance for one year, was available to the children and spouses of all employees who had been working at 84 Lumber or Nemacolin Woodlands Resort for at least two years.[45] Spouses and children of 10-year employees were eligible for the Eileen Jurofcik Memorial Scholarship, which was awarded annually to one outstanding individual and provided assistance for four years.[46]

Finally, children or spouses of any associate who had been with the company at least 20 years automatically received a $1,000 scholarship to help fund their education.[47] Outside of 84 Lumber, Hardy also donated money to California University of Pennsylvania and West Virginia University, creating scholarships named for his wife Debbie and daughters Paige and Taylor.[48]

Hardy was also interested in supporting education on a larger scale. After receiving an honorary degree from Washington and Jefferson College in 1984,[49] Hardy began to think about the ways in which he could make a positive contribution to the school. He decided that one thing he knew a great deal about was the entrepreneurial spirit. Accordingly, in 1987 Hardy established the Entrepreneurial Studies program at the college to encourage those qualities.[50]

Hardy also established the Joseph A. Hardy Jr. award in 1990 in honor of his son.[51] The scholarship was awarded to W & J juniors who demonstrated leadership, vision, and an excellent academic record.[52] The Joseph A. Hardy Sr. professorship in Economics and Entrepreneurial studies was also created.[53]

A NATURAL PARTNERSHIP

ALTHOUGH 84 LUMBER HAD WORKED with a variety of charities over the years, one of its most fruitful continuing partnerships was with Habitat for Humanity, an international organization that helps to provide affordable housing for low-income families.[1]

Since its founding in 1976, Habitat for Humanity International has built or renovated more than 50,000 houses in the United States, and more than 100,000 homes in countries around the world.[2] Hardy first took an interest in the charity after meeting with former U.S. President Jimmy Carter, a strong supporter of the charity.[3]

The connection between Habitat for Humanity and 84 Lumber was a natural one for many reasons. A building supplies retailer and a home-building charity are ideally suited to work together. But Habitat for Humanity also supports a strong work ethic, similar to Joe Hardy's.

Recipients are not simply given their new houses. They must devote hundreds of hours of volunteer work to the organization and pay for the supplies and the land used to build their homes.[4] Habitat for Humanity helps by providing volunteers and professional construction consultants to build the homes, selling them at cost, and arranging no-interest mortgage payments.[5]

One of the largest collaborations between 84 Lumber and Habitat for Humanity was the

84-Hour House, built in 1994. Judy Donohue, former publicist for 84 Lumber, first conceived of the idea, when she suggested to Joe Hardy that the two organizations team up to build a house in 84 days and christen it the 84 House.[6] Donohue recalled that Hardy decided the project should be more ambitious.

Upon hearing her proposal he declared, "They can build it in 84 hours. If they build it in 84 hours, I'll give them everything they need."[7]

On September 8, 1994, a team of volunteers began tackling the daunting assignment.[8] Over the course of the project, 600 volunteers, working in shifts, would lend a hand to construct the three-bedroom home[9] being built for Mellownee Merchant, a young mother who had been working with Habitat for Humanity for two years.[10]

Because Merchant was disabled and used a wheelchair, she needed a very specific type of house.[11] Habitat purchased an empty lot in Pittsburgh's Wilkinsburg neighborhood, and thanks to 84 Lumber, Merchant had a brand-new home that was built to meet her needs in just four days.[12] The workers successfully met the 84-hour deadline, and Merchant, her son, and her mother moved into the house soon afterward.[13]

84 Lumber continued to work with Habitat for Humanity branches across the country, donating supplies to build homes for needy families. In 2003, 84 Lumber donated nearly $184,000 to Habitat for Humanity homes, and the contributions continued.[14]

For example, in 2004, 84 Lumber donated over $6,000 to help a Habitat for Humanity branch in Elizabethtown, Kentucky, to construct a single-family home for another disabled parent.[15] The company also donated $15,000 to the greater Indianapolis-area Habitat for Humanity, which planned to build 28 new homes during the year.[16]

Many 84 Lumber employees have helped build Habitat for Humanity houses, and both the volunteers and Habitat for Humanity workers said they benefited greatly from the partnership.

Top: Joe Hardy became interested in Habitat for Humanity after meeting with former President Jimmy Carter.

Middle: 84 Lumber employee volunteers for a Habitat for Humanity project.

Bottom: Mellownee Merchant, center, of Wilkinsburg, Pennsylvania, her mother, and son were the recipients of the "84-Hour House." Also pictured are Habitat for Humanity construction supervisor Jim Kiggins, left, Joe Hardy, back, and Dick Weber, right.

In addition to their long-term charitable commitments, Joe Hardy and Maggie Hardy Magerko were always open to new ideas and one-time charitable requests. When Private Jessica Lynch, a soldier who was captured and injured during Operation Iraqi Freedom in 2003, prepared to return to her home in West Virginia, 84 Lumber donated $12,000 worth of materials to "Jessi's Home Project,"[54] which aimed to renovate the Lynch home to make it more accessible to the P.O.W. as she recovered from the injuries she sustained in combat.[55]

In another instance, Maggie Hardy Magerko stepped in to help rebuild a playground in New Brighton, Pennsylvania, that had been destroyed by an arsonist.[56] After hearing about the fire on the news, Hardy Magerko contacted New Brighton Mayor Paul Spickerman to offer her help.[57] She visited the playground with a team of 84 Lumber managers and pledged to donate the materials needed to repair the damage.[58] Furthermore, she rounded up a crew of volunteers to help rebuild the playground structures.[59]

In 2003, Maggie Hardy Magerko was fielding almost 300 requests for charitable donations every week.[60] When a reporter with the Uniontown, Pennsylvania, *Herald-Standard* asked her why she devoted so much time to charitable causes, she said:

> *We do a lot for different causes, different groups. I could easily ignore it, but... as I get satisfaction out of seeing people develop, I feel the same with donations. When I lie in bed at night, I think "Did I do anything to help anyone today? An associate, customer, a guest? Did I do anything to change the world?" In the position I'm in with these resources, it makes me feel good. I don't do it for media attention. For many years, this was done behind closed doors.*[61]

Evidently, her father felt the same way. Proud of the enormous successes he had achieved in business, he decided to help a new generation of young entrepreneurs down the same path. Friends reported that Hardy often gave money to young people planning to start their own businesses,[63] as well as a variety of other anonymous donations.

"You can have castles," he said. "It's people [that matter]."[64]

A Tenacious Spirit

Hardy once joked, "I think if I worked for a real company, they'd have gotten rid of me."[65]

While Hardy's business tactics have often seemed unusual and sometimes unpopular, his unwavering belief that nothing is impossible helped him grow a five-man lumberyard into a $3 billion-a-year empire. In 2004, the company ranked as the nation's largest privately held building materials supplier, with more than 500 stores, 16 component manufacturing plants, and 8,000 employees.[66]

Since Hardy turned the company on its heels in the early 1990s with his decision to shift the company's focus from home-improvement consumers to professional builders, 84 Lumber increased sales from $600 million to $3 billion, surviving the challenge from big-box retailers that had bankrupted so many others in the industry.

In an interview with the University of Pittsburgh's *Pitt* magazine, Chief Operating Officer Bill Myrick noted that in just 13 years the company had made a 180-degree turnaround from 1991, when it made 90 percent of its sales to homeowners, to 2004, when 90 percent of customers were professionals. By that

time, the cash-and-carry lumberyard that changed the way builders bought their supplies had topped $2 billion in accounts receivables, which accounted for about 00 percent of its business.[67]

According to company President Maggie Hardy Magerko, these successes, along with a more mature relationship with the homebuilding industry, have given the company the confidence to continue expanding.[68] In 2004, the company opened 18 new stores,[69] several of which are located in large, metropolitan markets where 84 Lumber stores had been forced to close in the past.[70] 84 Lumber's five-year plan included opening 50 to 60 new stores a year, and projected growth areas focused on manufactured products and install sales.[71]

As 84 Lumber approached its 50th year in business, those close to Hardy reflected on what exactly had fueled the company's rise to the top. Many believed that it was all due to Hardy himself. Some said that it was his ability to size up people, determine their best qualities, and encourage them to reach their full potential. Associates said that Hardy had a knack for selecting and promoting

Above: Maggie Hardy Magerko, center, visits the site of a playground in New Brighton, Pennsylvania, that was destroyed by an arsonist.

Right: 84 Lumber donated the materials and recruited volunteers to help rebuild the playground.

Opposite: Joe Hardy presents a donation to a city police department in 1999.

job candidates who would become dedicated, innovative, and hardworking employees.

84 Lumber associate Bill Fulton said, "Joe Hardy did surround himself with good people. ... That's what made it a good environment to work in, because you were working with... good, solid, hardworking people."[72]

Once employed at 84 Lumber, employees said, Joe Hardy did whatever he could to help them succeed and work their way up to greater responsibilities and rewards.

"The big thing with Joe is he stimulates the best in everybody. I mean he really does. He can pick out the weakness and make it a strength. I admire the man," said Install Sales Manager Bob

Opposite: Associates describe Joe Hardy as a hands–on employer who encourages them to find creative solutions to the challenges of business.

Right: An 84 Lumber associate restocks a display. In 2004, the company had more than 7,000 employees.

Below: In 2004, the company was the nation's largest privately held building materials supplier, with 453 stores in 35 states.

MacKinney, who had worked at 84 Lumber for almost four decades.[73]

According to Jack Klema, who built hundreds of lumber stores and other buildings for 84 Lumber over the years, "Joe was always encouraging [us] to figure out better ways. ... If there [was]... a better way to do anything, [or] you wanted to try something different... he was always for it."[74]

Dean Martik, whose family business was often called upon to do remodeling work at 84 Lumber stores, Nemacolin Woodlands Resort, as well as the Hardy family's personal properties, said that despite Hardy's reputation as a demanding employer, he was never difficult to work with.

"I remember everybody always said how hard they are to work for, especially Joe," he said. "We've never had a problem with them. ... We know what they expect because we've been working for them [for so long]."[75]

Jeanene Tomshay, a 30-year employee, added, "He's such a great teacher, and at the time, you may not think so. You might be thinking, 'Oh, my God. ... He's getting all fired up.' But the fire in him is transferred to you. It's the transference that makes

Opposite: Hardy takes time out for a break with vendor representative Ed Robb.

Left: *The Eagle* interviews Hardy at a grand opening. In 2004, the company had plans to open 25 new 84 Lumber stores a year.

Below: Employees said they always found Joe Hardy to be approachable.

you alive and makes you take on doing things that 84 needs."[76]

Employees also noted that Hardy helped build their confidence by giving them so much responsibility. Dan Wallach said that whenever a problem arose, Hardy expected the associate who informed him about it to already be formulating a possible solution.[77]

Sid McAllister, a former chief financial officer at 84 Lumber who later did computer and financial consulting for the company, said Hardy was willing to consider any solution that would benefit the company, even if it temporarily bruised his own ego. McAllister remembered a time when he was planning to approach Hardy with the news that eight money-losing stores in California should be closed.

"Everybody was convinced I was going to get fired because I was going to broach that subject with Joe, because it would just kill him to close a store," McAllister said. He remembered opening the discussion by telling Hardy that he knew of an "opportunity" for the company to make a couple million dollars a year, although it might be painful for Hardy. After hearing the facts, Hardy's quick response was, "Close them."[78]

Learning Made it Fun

Hardy had always been an extremely demanding boss, insisting that his employees be willing to work the same overtime hours and make the same cross-country treks that he himself had been committed to throughout the history of the company. But associates agreed that Hardy was a fair employer, and that anyone willing to provide the hard work Hardy asked for would receive ample rewards.

MacKinney, speaking for himself and Gail Baughman, another long-time employee, explained, "We found a company that treats you really fairly, and Joe has set goals that you have to attain, and really, he always keeps you trying to better yourself and trying to better the company."[79]

Debbie Hardy, an employee who started in an entry-level job and worked her way up to a managerial position, added, "Anyone that ever walks away from 84 Lumber... that doesn't learn something, there's something wrong with them. Because

Joe Hardy poses with a group of 84 Lumber employees. Associates who had worked at the company for many years said they stayed because they were always treated with respect and given opportunities for advancement.

at 84 Lumber… you have so many opportunities just waiting."[80]

It is no surprise, then, that some employees stayed with 84 Lumber for decades. The associates who had known him the longest had a deep-seated affection for Hardy and unflagging loyalty to the company he built.

Cecil Gravely, who joined 84 Lumber in 1967, remarked, "People tell me that Joe Hardy is a tough man, but he's a good man. … He respects you, [and] he's got a heart of gold."[81]

Tomshay said that, even after retiring, she still felt a strong connection to the company. "I still feel

[like] part of the 84 team, and every year, when I give out the Jeanene Tomshay Award at the awards banquet… I say the 84 blood that runs through my veins is Pantone No. 485 Red, which is the color of the 84 logo."[82]

But of all of Hardy's stand-out qualities, friends and associates were most impressed by the extraordinary level of energy and constant drive that he possessed.

Jerry Maley, Debbie Hardy's father, remarked, "The man really sits back and pays attention, and he gathers thoughts in his mind. He just gathers information. He reminds you of some brilliant 16- or 17-year-old… [whose] mind is starving for knowledge. He's like that at 80 years old."[83]

Hardy's grandson, Alex Hardy, added, "Gramp is 20 times busier today than he… was 20 years ago."[84]

Although his daughter Maggie Hardy Magerko had taken on a large part of the job of operating and expanding 84 Lumber, Joe Hardy had run his business for years with an iron fist, a tight control on finances, and scrupulous attention to detail.

At the same time, he never forgot to send cards to his employees on important occasions such as their birthdays and anniversaries. Hardy had made his mark as both a lumber baron and a common man, someone who employees said was always approachable.

Hardy himself had his own theories about why he had been successful. One was his refusal to accept obstacles of any kind. Over the years, he had shown a commitment to attack any problem with dogged determination. At times, he had to set aside the feelings of friends and associates in order pursue his single-minded vision, but it had usually served him well.

"If he could dream it, it wasn't impossible," said Greg Clark, who joined the company in 1969 and was still there 35 years later. "He could make it happen."[85]

The other source of his success, Hardy believed, was his ongoing zest for life and continual quest for knowledge. For Joe Hardy, the job was never finished. He was always looking for the next step and a new adventure to embark upon. His relentless pursuit of success and personal betterment kept him sharp and helped him to run rings around employees half his age.

Looking ahead to the future, Joe Hardy remarked, "Anyplace I go, it's not to enjoy myself. My enjoyment is to see if I can't steal an idea. ... Learn, learn, learn. You keep learning. That makes it fun."[86]

NOTES TO SOURCES

Chapter One

1. Joe Hardy III, interview by Jeffrey L. Rodengen, audio recording, 1 October 2003, Write Stuff Enterprises.
2. Stefan Lorant, *Pittsburgh: The Story of an American City* (Lenox, MA: Authors Edition, Inc., 1975), 333.
3. Ibid.
4. Ibid., 335.
5. Ibid.
6. Ibid., 336.
7. Ibid.
8. Ibid., 322.
9. Ibid.
10. Ibid., 340.
11. Ibid.
12. Ibid., 343.
13. Ibid.
14. Ibid., 348.
15. Joe Hardy III, interview, 1 October 2003.
16. Robert Hardy, interview by Jeffrey L. Rodengen, 30 September 2003, Write Stuff Enterprises.
17. Ibid.
18. Joe Hardy III, interview, 1 October 2003.
19. Ibid.
20. Robert Hardy, interview.
21. Ibid.
22. Ibid.
23. Ibid.
24. Joe Hardy III, interview, 1 October 2003.
25. Ibid.
26. Ibid.
27. Ibid.
28. Ibid.
29. Ibid.
30. Ibid.
31. Ibid.
32. Robert Hardy, interview.
33. Ibid.
34. Joe Hardy III, interview, 1 October 2003.
35. Ibid.
36. Ibid.
37. Lorant, *Pittsburgh*, 371.

Chapter Two

1. Joe Hardy III, interview, 1 October 2003.
2. Ibid.
3. Ibid.
4. Robert Hardy, interview.
5. Ibid.
6. Ibid.
7. Joe Hardy III, interview, 1 October 2003.
8. Ibid.
9. Robert Hardy, interview.
10. Joe Hardy III, interview, 1 October 2003.
11. Robert Hardy, interview.
12. Ibid.
13. Joe Hardy III, interview, 1 October 2003.
14. Ibid.
15. Ibid.
16. Ibid.
17. Edward Ryan, interview by Jeffrey L. Rodengen, audio recording, 1 October 2003, Write Stuff Enterprises.
18. Joe Hardy III, interview, 1 October 2003.
19. Ibid.
20. Nan Cameron, interview by Jeffrey L. Rodengen, audio recording, 30 September 2003, Write Stuff Enterprises.
21. Robert Hardy, interview.
22. Ibid.
23. Ibid.
24. Edward Ryan, interview.
25. "Memories: A 60th Birthday Tribute to Joe Hardy," letter from Edward Crump III, 84 Lumber Co., 7 January 1983.

26. "Memories," letter from Dale Armstrong.
27. Ibid.
28. Cameron, interview.
29. Ibid.
30. Ibid.
31. Ibid.
32. Ibid.
33. Ibid.
34. Ibid.
35. Ibid.
36. Ibid.
37. Joe Hardy III, interview, 1 October 2003.
38. Ibid.
39. Ibid.
40. Ibid.
41. Ibid.
42. Robert Hardy, interview.
43. Ibid.
44. Ibid.
45. Ibid.
46. Ibid.
47. Joe Hardy III, interview, 1 October 2003.
48. Edward Ryan, interview.
49. Lorant, *Pittsburgh*, 370-371.
50. Ibid., 374.
51. Ibid., 377.
52. Ibid., 378-379.
53. Ibid., 386.
54. Ibid., 425-426.
55. Ibid., 417.
56. "Memories," letter from Newton Teichman.
57. Joe Hardy III, interview, 1 October 2003.
58. Edward Ryan, interview.
59. Ibid.
60. Ibid.
61. Joe Hardy III, interview, 1 October 2003.
62. Ibid.
63. Ibid.
64. Joseph Alexander Hardy V, interview by Jeffrey L. Rodengen, audio recording, 1 October 2003, Write Stuff Enterprises.
65. Ibid.
66. "Memories," letter from Teichman.
67. Ibid.

68. Ibid.
69. Robert Hardy, interview.
70. Ibid.
71. Ibid.
72. Ibid.
73. Ibid.
74. Joe Hardy III, interview, 1 October 2003.
75. Ibid.
76. Ibid.
77. Ibid.
78. Edward Ryan, interview.
79. Joe Hardy III, interview, 1 October 2003.

Chapter Three

1. Robert Hardy, interview.
2. Joe Hardy III, interview, 1 October 2003.
3. Ibid.
4. Ibid.
5. Edward Ryan, interview.
6. Ibid.
7. Ibid.
8. Ibid.
9. Joe Hardy III, interview, 1 October 2003.
10. Ibid.
11. Ibid.
12. Edward Ryan, interview.
13. Ibid.
14. Ibid.
15. Joe Hardy III, interview, 1 October 2003.
16. Edward Ryan, interview.
17. Virginia Hackman, interview by Jeffrey L. Rodengen, audio recording, 26 October 2004, Write Stuff Enterprises.
18. Joe Hardy III, interview, 1 October 2003.
19. Ibid.
20. Ibid.
21. Ibid.
22. Ibid.
23. Ibid.
24. Ibid.
25. Ibid.
26. Ibid.
27. Ibid.
28. Robert Hardy, interview.
29. Edward Ryan, interview.

30. Joe Hardy III, interview, 1 October 2003.
31. Ibid.
32. Ibid.
33. Ibid.
34. Ibid.
35. Ibid.
36. Cecil Gravely, interview by Richard F. Hubbard, audio recording, 8 December 2003, Write Stuff Enterprises.
37. Edward Ryan, interview.
38. Joe Hardy III, interview, 1 October 2003.
39. Robert Hardy, interview.
40. Ibid.
41. Joe Hardy III, interview, 1 October 2003.
42. Ibid.
43. Donna Criss, interview by Richard F. Hubbard, audio recording, 1 October 2003, Write Stuff Enterprises.
44. Ibid.
45. Ibid.
46. Ibid.
47. Ibid.
48. Ibid.
49. Bud and Helen Dofi, interview by Richard F. Hubbard, audio recording, 9 December 2003, Write Stuff Enterprises.
50. Ibid.
51. Ibid.
52. Ibid.
53. Ibid.
54. Ibid.
55. Ibid.
56. Ibid.
57. Ibid.
58. Ibid.
59. Ibid.
60. Willis Able, interview by Jeffrey L. Rodengen, audio recording, 23 February 2005, Write Stuff Enterprises.
61. Robert Hardy, interview.
62. Ibid.
63. Ibid.
64. William Conover, interview by Richard F. Hubbard, audio recording,

1 October 2003,
Write Stuff Enterprises.
65. Ibid.
66. Ibid.
67. Ibid.
68. Ibid.
69. Edward Ryan, interview.
70. Robert Hardy, interview.

Chapter Three Sidebar:
Ed Ryan Fuels Family's Love
of Building

1. "William Ryan Homes,"
American Builders Network,
http://americanbuilders.com/
WRH
2. Ibid.
3. Ibid.
4. Ibid.
5. Joe Hardy III, interview,
1 October 2003.
6. William J. Ryan, interview
by Anjali Sachdeva,
13 August 2004,
Write Stuff Enterprises.
7. Ibid.
8. Ibid.
9. "William Ryan Homes."
10. "Ryan Homes, Inc. Collection,"
Carnegie Mellon University
Libraries,
http://www.library.cmu.edu/
Research/ArchArch/
ryanhome.html
11. Ibid.
12. Ibid.
13. Ibid.
14. Ibid.
15. Ibid.
16. Ibid.
17. Ibid.
18. Ibid.
19. Ibid.
20. "About Ryan Homes," Ryan
Homes, www.ryanhomes.com
21. Ibid.
22. Ibid.
23. Allen Norwood, "Ryan
Homes Ranks No. 1 for
Customer Satisfaction,"
The Charlotte Observer
(online edition),
3 October 2003.

24. William J. Ryan, interview.
25. "Building Value for Three
Generation," Ryan
Building Group,
http://www.ryanbldgrp.com/
aboutthegroup.asp
26. William J. Ryan, interview.

Chapter Four

1. Joe Hardy III, interview, 1
October 2003.
2. Ibid.
3. Ibid.
4. Ibid.
5. Ibid.
6. Ibid.
7. Ibid.
8. Ibid.
9. Ibid.
10. Ibid.
11. Ibid.
12. Ibid.
13. Robert Hardy, interview.
14. Ibid.
15. Ibid.
16. Joe Hardy III, interview, 1
October 2003.
17. Ibid.
18. Robert Hardy, interview.
19. Ibid.
20. Ibid.
21. "Timber!" Pennsylvania
Lumber Museum Online,
http://www.lumbermuseum.o
rg/history.html
22. Ibid.
23. Ibid.
24. Robert Hardy, interview.
25. Joe Hardy III, interview, 1
October 2003.
26. Robert Hardy, interview.
27. Ibid.
28. Conover, interview.
29. Robert Hardy, interview.
30. Ibid.
31. Ibid.
32. Charles Moore, interview
by Richard F. Hubbard,
audio recording,
17 December 2003,
Write Stuff Enterprises.
33. Barb Mosi, interview
by Richard F. Hubbard,

audio recording,
30 September 2003,
Write Stuff Enterprises.
34. Ibid.
35. Joe Hardy III, interview,
1 October 2003.
36. Ibid.
37. Ibid.
38. Ibid.
39. Moore, interview.
40. Gail Baughman, interview
by Richard F. Hubbard,
audio recording,
1 October 2003,
Write Stuff Enterprises.
41. Robert Hardy, interview.
42. Ibid.
43. Moore, interview.
44. Ibid.
45. Robert Hardy, interview.
46. Ibid.
47. Joe Hardy III, interview,
1 October 2003.
48. Ibid.

Chapter Four Sidebar:
Origin of Town's Name Still a Mystery

1. "Facts About 84,"
84 Lumber Co.,
http://www.84lumber.com/
About84/Facts_About_84/
Why84_2.asp.
2. Patrick Connors, *Historic
Towns of Washington County*
(Monongahela, Pennsylvania:
Historic Towns Publishing,
n.d.), 21.
3. Ibid.
4. Ibid.
5. Ibid.
6. Ibid.
7. Ibid.
8. "Facts About 84,"
84 Lumber Co.
9. Ibid.
10. Ibid.
11. Ibid.
12. Ibid.

Chapter Five

1. Joe Hardy III, interview,
1 October 2003.

2. Ibid.
3. Ibid.
4. Robert Hardy, interview.
5. Joe Hardy III, interview,
   1 October 2003.
6. Moore, interview.
7. Maggie Hardy Magerko,
   interview by
   Jeffrey L. Rodengen,
   audio recording,
   12 July 2004, Write Stuff
   Enterprises.
8. Betty Gottschalk, interview
   by Jeffrey L. Rodengen,
   audio recording,
   12 July 2004,
   Write Stuff Enterprises.
9. Conover, interview.
10. Joseph Alexander Hardy V,
    interview.
11. Ibid.
12. Ibid.
13. Joe Hardy III, interview
    by Jeffrey L. Rodengen,
    audio recording,
    12 July 2004,
    Write Stuff Enterprises.
14. Joseph Alexander Hardy V,
    interview.
15. Conover, interview.
16. Hardy Magerko, interview.
17. Joe Hardy III, interview,
    1 October 2003.
18. Ibid.
19. Ibid.
20. Ibid.
21. Ibid.
22. Ibid.
23. Jack Knight, Esq.,
    interview by
    Richard F. Hubbard,
    audio recording,
    18 February 2004,
    Write Stuff Enterprises.
24. Jeanene M. Tomshay,
    interview by Jeffrey L.
    Rodengen, audio
    recording, 1 October 2003,
    Write Stuff Enterprises.
25. Ibid.
26. Ibid.
27. Ibid.
28. Dan Hixenbaugh, interview
    by Richard F. Hubbard,

audio recording,
   4 December 2003,
   Write Stuff Enterprises.
29. Gravely, interview.
30. Ibid.
31. Ibid.
32. Ibid.
33. Baughman, interview.
34. Ibid.
35. Ibid.
36. Ibid.
37. Ibid.
38. Ibid.
39. Ibid.
40. Ibid.
41. Ibid.
42. Conover, interview.
43. Baughman, interview.
44. Ibid.
45. Ibid.
46. Ibid.
47. Rose Pournaras, interview
    by Jeffrey L. Rodengen,
    audio recording,
    2 December 2004,
    Write Stuff Enterprises.
48. Chris Pournaras, interview
    by Jeffrey L. Rodengen,
    audio recording,
    2 December 2004,
    Write Stuff Enterprises.
49. Dan Wallach, interview
    by Jeffrey L. Rodengen,
    audio recording,
    12 July 2004,
    Write Stuff Enterprises.
50. Tomshay, interview.
51. Ibid.
52. Ibid.
53. Ibid.
54. Ibid.
55. Hixenbaugh, interview.
56. Tomshay, interview.
57. Hixenbaugh, interview.
58. Bob MacKinney, interview
    by Richard F. Hubbard,
    audio recording,
    1 October 2003,
    Write Stuff Enterprises.
59. Ibid.
60. Ibid.
61. Tomshay, interview.
62. Ibid.
63. Ibid.

64. Ibid.
65. Ibid.
66. Ibid.
67. Ibid.
68. Ibid.
69. Robin Freed, interview
    by Richard F. Hubbard,
    audio recording,
    4 December 2003,
    Write Stuff Enterprises.
70. Ibid.
71. Ibid.
72. Conover, interview.
73. Robert Hardy, interview.
74. Joe Hardy III, interview,
    1 October 2003.
75. Tomshay, interview.
76. Hixenbaugh, interview.
77. Moore, interview.
78. Robert Hardy, interview.
79. Hixenbaugh, interview.
80. Moore, interview.
81. Ibid.
82. Ibid.
83. Hixenbaugh, interview.
84. Bill Fulton, interview
    by Richard F. Hubbard,
    audio recording,
    2 December 2003,
    Write Stuff Enterprises.
85. Moore, interview.
86. Barbara Stork, interview
    by Jeffrey L. Rodengen,
    audio recording,
    1 October 2003,
    Write Stuff Enterprises.
87. Hixenbaugh, interview.
88. Ibid.
89. Ibid.
90. Ibid.
91. Ibid.
92. Ibid.
93. Ibid.
94. Moore, interview.
95. Mike Figgins, interview
    by Jeffrey L. Rodengen,
    audio recording,
    2 December 2004,
    Write Stuff Enterprises.
96. Terry Carter, interview
    by Jeffrey L. Rodengen,
    audio recording,
    1 October 2003,
    Write Stuff Enterprises.

Chapter Five Sidebar:
Signs Point the Way to 84 Lumber

1. Hixenbaugh, interview.
2. Judy Donohue, interview by Richard F. Hubbard, audio recording, 3 December 2003, Write Stuff Enterprises.
3. Moore, interview.
4. Donohue, interview.
5. Stork, interview.
6. Ibid.
7. Donohue, interview.
8. Carter, interview.
9. Donohue, interview.

Chapter Six

1. Bud Weber, interview by Richard F. Hubbard, audio recording, 1 October 2003, Write Stuff Enterprises.
2. Baughman, interview.
3. Ray Barley, interview by Richard F. Hubbard, audio recording, 1 October 2003, Write Stuff Enterprises.
4. Phil Drake, interview by Jeffrey L. Rodengen, audio recording, 5 November 2004, Write Stuff Enterprises.
5. Bill Myrick, interview by Jeffrey L. Rodengen, audio recording, 15 October 2004, Write Stuff Enterprises.
6. Weber, interview.
7. Jim Zaunick, interview by Jeffrey L. Rodengen, audio recording, 30 September 2003, Write Stuff Enterprises.
8. Tomshay, interview.
9. Wallach, interview.
10. Denny Brua, interview by Richard F. Hubbard, audio recording, 3 December 2003, Write Stuff Enterprises.
11. Bob Hardy, interview.
12. Brua, interview.
13. Bob Hardy, interview.
14. Brua, interview.
15. Ibid.
16. Ibid.
17. Ibid.
18. Ibid.
19. Ibid.
20. Bernie Magerko, interview by Richard F. Hubbard, audio recording, 3 December 2003, Write Stuff Enterprises.
21. Barley, interview.
22. Bob Martik, interview by Richard F. Hubbard, audio recording, 19 February 2004, Write Stuff Enterprises.
23. Barley, interview.
24. Nick Ludi, interview by Jeffrey L. Rodengen, audio recording, 12 July 2004, Write Stuff Enterprises.
25. Zaunick, interview.
26. Greg Clark, interview by Jeffrey L. Rodengen, audio recording, 6 December 2004, Write Stuff Enterprises.
27. Barley, interview.
28. Ibid.
29. Gravely, interview.
30. Harry Zeune, interview by Richard F. Hubbard, audio recording, 5 December 2003, Write Stuff Enterprises.
31. Ibid.
32. James Funyak, interview by Jeffrey L. Rodengen, audio recording, 8 December 2004, Write Stuff Enterprises.
33. Jerry King, interview by Jeffrey L. Rodengen, audio recording, 7 December 2004, Write Stuff Enterprises.
34. Stork, interview.
35. Ibid.
36. Joseph Alexander Hardy V, interview.
37. Ibid.
38. Ibid.
39. Ibid.
40. Freed, interview.
41. Bob Hardy, interview.
42. Ibid.
43. Ibid.
44. Ibid.
45. Ibid.
46. Ibid.
47. Cameron, interview.
48. Edward Ryan, interview.
49. David Templeton, "Dorothy Pierce Hardy: Prominent Horse Breeder, Socialite, Volunteer," *Pittsburgh Post-Gazette*, 6 December 2002, B.
50. Baughman, interview.
51. Ibid.
52. Ibid.
53. Ibid.
54. Ibid.
55. Moore, interview.
56. Ibid.
57. Dolfi, interview.
58. Frank Cicero, interview by Jeffrey L. Rodengen, audio recording, 12 July 2004, Write Stuff Enterprises.
59. Paul Lentz, telephone interview by Amy Bush, 4 May 2005, Write Stuff Enterprises.
60. Baughman, interview.
61. Barley, interview.
62. Weber, interview.
63. Bill Underdonk, interview by Jeffrey L. Rodengen, audio recording, 27 October 2004, Write Stuff Enterprises.
64. Cheri Bomar, interview by Jeffrey L. Rodengen, audio recording, 12 July 2004, Write Stuff Enterprises.
65. Moore, interview.
66. Wallach, interview.
67. Hackman, interview.
68. Nancy Young, interview by Jeffrey L. Rodengen, audio recording, 27 October 2004, Write Stuff Enterprises.

69. Joe Hardy III, interview,
1 October 2003.

**Chapter Six Sidebar:
"84 U" Helps Managers Excel**

1. Hixenbaugh, interview.
2. Ibid.
3. Tomshay, interview.
4. Hixenbaugh, interview.
5. Ibid.
6. Tomshay, interview.
7. Ibid.

Chapter Seven

1. "Lights, Camera, Action!", *84
Family News*, October 1980.
2. Ibid.
3. Ibid.
4. "84 Lumber Aims for No. 1 with
a Billion-Dollar Blitz,"
Business Week, 9 July 1984.
5. Ibid.
6. Ibid.
7. Drake, interview.
8. Ibid.
9. Ibid.
10. Ibid.
11. Ibid.
12. Ibid.
13. Ibid.
14. *84 Family News*, April 1984.
15. "84 Lumber, Just the Facts,"
company document,
January 1991.
16. "The Start of a Grand Year,"
84 Family News, April 1984.
17. "84 Lumber, Biography:
Joseph A. Hardy, Sr.,"
company document,
January 1991.
18. Ibid.
19. "Homes in a Kit," *Changing
Times*, August 1981.
20. Joe Donaldson,
"Live It Up in the
House You Built,"
Niagara Falls, NY Gazette,
22 July 1981.
21. Ibid.
22. Ibid.
23. Ibid.
24. Drake, interview.

25. Joseph Alexander Hardy V,
interview.
26. "Glossary," National Multiple
Sclerosis Society,
www.nationalmssociety.org
27. "What is Multiple
Sclerosis?" National
Multiple Sclerosis Society,
www.nationalmssociety.org
28. Ibid.
29. Joseph Alexander Hardy V,
interview.
30. Joe Hardy III, interview,
1 October 2003.
31. Joseph Alexander Hardy V,
interview.
32. Ibid.
33. Ibid.
34. Ibid.
35. Ibid.
36. "84 Rides High on its
Low-Brow Approach,"
ProSales, May 1991.
37. Ibid.
38. Ibid.
39. Danel Bates, "On the Cheap,"
Small Business News
(Columbus, Ohio),
July 1995.
40. Ibid.
41. Ibid.
42. Ibid.
43. Ibid.
44. "84: The American Dream,"
Passport to Pittsburgh, 1993.
45. "FAQs," Nemacolin Woodlands,
www.nemacolin.com
46. "About Us," Nemacolin
Woodslands,
www.nemacolin.com
47. Ibid.
48. Ibid.
49. Ibid.
50. Ibid.
51. Ibid.
52. Andrew Wilson,
"Maggie Hardy Magerko
Making Plans for
Nemacolin, 84 Lumber,"
Allegheny Business News,
January 1993.
53. John Caulfield, "84 Lumber's
Joe Hardy Still Seeking
New Challenges," *National

Home Center News*,
24 April 1989, 17.
54. Cameron, interview.
55. Ibid.
56. Ibid.
57. Ibid.
58. Ibid.
59. Ibid.
60. Ibid.
61. Ibid.
62. Ibid.
63. Ibid
64. Joe Hardy III, interview,
1 October 2003.
66. MacKinney, interview.
67. Craig Johnson, interview
by Richard F. Hubbard,
audio recording,
3 December 2003,
Write Stuff Enterprises.
68. Ibid.
69. Ibid.
70. Don Gearhart, interview
by Richard F. Hubbard,
audio recording,
19 February 2004,
Write Stuff Enterprises.
71. Ibid.
72. Ibid.
73. Caulfield, "84 Lumber's
Joe Hardy," 17.
74. Ibid, 18.
75. Ibid.
76. Ibid.
77. Ibid.
78. Joe Hardy III, interview,
1 October 2003.

Chapter Eight

1. "Dealer 100," *ProSales*,
May/June 1992.
2. Andrew Page, "84 Lumber
Climbs Past Competition
to the Top,"
National Home Center News,
9 June 1997.
3. Jim McCorkle, interview
by Jeffrey L. Rodengen,
audio recording,
9 December 2004,
Write Stuff Enterprises.
4. Page, "84 Lumber Climbs
Past Competition."

5. *84 Family News*, July 1992.
6. Ibid.
7. Joyce Gannon, "Bargain Basements," *Pittsburgh Post-Gazette*, 11 April 1992.
8. Christie Campbell, "84 Lumber Moves into Prepackaged Homes," *Observer-Reporter* (Washington, Pennsylvania), 13 February 1993.
9. "Hurricane Andrew 1992," National Oceanic and Atmospheric Administration, www.publicaffairs.noaa.gov
10. "84 Lumber Celebrates 200th Store Opening," *Qualified Remodeler*, 1 November 1997.
11. Walter E. Johnson, "Life at 84 Lumber," *Do-It-Yourself Retailing*, February 1992.
12. "84 Lumber Training Center," *Observer-Reporter* (Washington, Pennsylvania), 17 November 1991.
13. Ibid.
14. Cicero, interview, 12 July 2004.
15. Jim Guest, interview by Jeffrey L. Rodengen, audio recording, 2 December 2004, Write Stuff Enterprises.
16. Mario Mullig, "Why Joe Hardy is No Longer on the Forbes List," *Observer-Reporter* (Washington, Pennsylvania), 11 October 1992.
17. Hardy Magerko, interview.
18. Mullig, "Why Joe Hardy is No Longer on the Forbes List."
19. Frances Borsodi Zajac, "For Resort President PGA Event's a Dream Come True," *Uniontown Herald-Standard*, 16 September 2003.
20. Mullig, "Why Joe Hardy is No Longer on the Forbes List."
21. Ibid.
22. Carter, interview.
23. Mullig, "Why Joe Hardy is No Longer on the Forbes List."
24. Hardy Magerko, interview.

25. Joe Hardy III, interview, 12 July 2004.
26. Christina Toras, interview by Jeffrey L. Rodengen, audio recording, 15 November 2004, Write Stuff Enterprises.
27. Dan Hixenbaugh, interview.
28. Debbie Hardy, interview by Richard F. Hubbard, audio recording, 1 October 2003, Write Stuff Enterprises.
29. Ibid.
30. Ibid.
31. Ibid.
32. Ibid.
33. Ibid.
34. Ibid.
35. Ibid.
36. Ibid.
37. Ibid.
38. Ibid.
39. Ibid.
40. Ibid.
41. Ibid.
42. Ibid.
43. Ibid.
44. Ibid.
45. Ibid.
46. Ibid.
47. Ibid.
48. Ibid.
49. Ibid.
50. Ibid.
51. Ibid.
52. Ibid.
53. Ibid.
54. Ibid.
55. Ibid.
56. Ibid.
57. Ibid.
58. Ibid.
59. Ibid.
60. Ibid.
61. Hardy Magerko, interview.
62. Hackman, interview.
63. Debbie Hardy, interview.
64. Hardy Magerko, interview.
65. Debbie Hardy, interview.
66. Zajac, "For Resort President."
67. Debbie Hardy, interview.
68. Zajac, "For Resort President."
69. Baughman, interview.
70. "84 Lumber Alters Image with Stylish Showrooms," National

Home Center News, 8 March 1999.
71. Ibid.
72. Ibid.
73. Ibid.
74. MacKinney, interview.
75. "84 Lumber Alters Image."
76. Ibid.
77. Ibid.
78. Jason Gonzalez, "84 Lumber Opens Second, Larger Maggie's Showroom," *National Home Center News*, 8 November 1999.
79. Ibid.
80. MacKinney, interview.
81. Ibid.
82. Ibid.
83. Baughman, interview.
84. Gonzalez, "84 Lumber Opens Second."

**Chapter Eight Sidebar:
Lord Hardy**

1. Gonzalez, "84 Lumber Opens Second."
2. Mark Belko, "Lumber Baron Becomes Lord of the Manor," *Pittsburgh Post-Gazette*, 27 July 1990.
3. Ibid.
4. Ibid.
5. Ibid.
6. Ibid.
7. Betty Rohlf, "An Afternoon of Pomp and Circumstance," *Uniontown Herald-Standard*, 4 August 1991.
8. Ibid.
9. Cathy Lubenski, "Joe Hardy Relinquishes Title as 'Lord of the Manor' to Daughter," *Sunday Tribune Review* (Greensburg, Pennsylvania), 3 September 1995.
10. Ibid.
11. Ibid.

Chapter Nine

1. Joe Hardy III, interview, 1 October 2003.
2. Ibid.

3. Teresa F. Lindeman, "If It's Wednesday, It Must Be Nevada, for 84 Lumber's Maggie Hardy Magerko," *Pittsburgh Post-Gazette*, 26 March 2002.

4. Janice Crompton, "Joe Hardy Rebuilding His Empire," *Pittsburgh Post-Gazette*, 30 May 1999.

5. Myrick, interview

6. Joe Hardy III, interview, 1 October 2003.

7. Lindeman, "If It's Wednesday."

8. King, interview.

9. Lindeman, "If It's Wednesday."

10. Ibid.

11. Hardy Magerko, interview.

12. Myrick, interview.

13. Crompton, "Joe Hardy Rebuilding."

14. Ibid.

15. "84 Lumber Unveils New Store Format," 84 Lumber news release, May 1999.

16. Jason Gonzalez, "84 Charges Ahead With Change," *National Home Center News*, 7 June 1999, 18.

17. Ibid.

18. Ibid.

19. Ibid.

20. Ibid.

21. "84 Lumber Unveils New Store Format."

22. Gonzalez, "84 Charges Ahead."

23. Ibid.

24. Ibid.

25. "84 Lumber Unveils New Store Format."

26. Hardy Magerko, interview.

27. Carter, interview.

28. Erica Gallagher, "From the Ground Up," *U.S. Business Review*, July 2002, 4.

29. "84 Lumber Company to Open Record 20 Stores on April 3, 2002," 84 Lumber news release, 21 March 2002.

30. Lindeman, "If It's Wednesday."

31. "84 Lumber Company to Open Record 20 Stores."

32. Ibid.

33. Hardy Magerko, interview.

34. "84 Lumber Company to Open Record 20 Stores."

35. Ibid.

36. Lindeman, "If It's Wednesday."

37. Carter, interview.

38. Lindeman, "If It's Wednesday."

39. Ibid.

40. Hardy Magerko, interview.

41. Gallagher, "From the Ground Up."

42. Lindeman, "If It's Wednesday."

43. Ibid.

44. "84 Lumber Surpasses $2 Billion in Sales," 84 Lumber news release, 9 December 2002.

45. Ibid.

46. Ibid.

47. Templeton, "Dorothy Pierce Hardy."

48. Hardy Magerko, interview.

49. Freed, interview.

50. "Press Room Timeline," Nemacolin Woodlands Resort and Spa Web site, www.nemacolin.com

51. Ibid.

52. Ibid.

53. Ibid.

54. Ibid.

55. Gearhart, interview.

56. "Press Room Timeline," Nemacolin Woodlands Resort and Spa Web site.

57. Ibid.

58. Ibid.

59. Ibid.

60. Jeff Kmiec, interview by Jeffrey L. Rodengen, audio recording, 12 July 2004, Write Stuff Enterprises.

61. Michelle Conlin, "Putting on the Ritz," *Forbes 400*, 12 October 1998.

62. Pete Magerko, interview by Jeffrey L. Rodengen, audio recording, 12 July 2004, Write Stuff Enterprises.

63. Conlin, "Putting on the Ritz."

64. Ibid.

65. Public relations department, Nemacolin Woodlands Resort and Spa, conversation with Anjali Sachdeva.

66. "Press Room Timeline," Nemacolin Woodlands Resort and Spa Web site.

67. Wanda Anker, interview by Jeffrey L. Rodengen, audio recording, 15 July 2004, Write Stuff Enterprises.

68. Ibid.

69. Trey Matheu, interview by Jeffrey L. Rodengen, audio recording, 14 July 2004, Write Stuff Enterprises.

70. "Press Room Timeline," Nemacolin Woodlands Resort and Spa Web site.

71. Ibid.

72. Ibid.

73. Ibid.

74. Ibid.

75. Ibid.

76. Gerry Dulac, "Golf 2003 Preview: The Lord of Mystic Rock," *Pittsburgh Post-Gazette*, 13 April 2003.

77. Dave Stofcheck, "Mutch, PGA Give Hardy, Mystic Rock High Marks," *Herald-Standard* (Uniontown, Pennsylvania), 16 September 2003.

78. Ibid.

79. Ibid.

80. Ibid.

81. Ibid.

82. Mike Ciarochi, "Bad Weather Halts Pro-am," *Herald-Standard* (Uniontown, Pennsylvania), 16 September 2003.

83. Ibid.

84. Rob Burchianti, " 'Hardyland' a Hit," *Herald-Standard* (Uniontown, Pennsylvania), 18 September 2003.

85. Ibid.

86. Ibid.

87. "Special Events," Nemacolin Woodlands Resort and Spa Web site, www.nemacolin.com

88. Dulac, "Golf 2003 Preview."

89. Jeff Kmiec, telephone interview by Amy Bush, 6 May 2005, Write Stuff Enterprises.

90. Jerry Maley, Sr., interview by Richard F. Hubbard, audio recording, 30 September 2003, Write Stuff Enterprises.
91. Anker, interview.

Chapter Nine Sidebar:
Chapel Honors Heroes of Flight 93

1. *Thunder on the Mountain: Flight 93 Memorial Chapel*, videocassette, produced and directed by Jon K. Miller, Valley Production Center (Bath, Pennsylvania), 2002.
2. Ibid.
3. Ibid.
4. Ibid.
5. Ibid.
6. Ibid.
7. Ibid.
8. Ibid.
9. Ibid.
10. Ibid.
11. Ibid.
12. "84 Lumber Donated Over $23,000 to the Flight 93 Memorial Chapel and to the Memory of Those Who Perished September 11, 2001," 84 Lumber news release, 23 August 2002.
13. Ibid.

Chapter Ten

1. Freed, interview.
2. Ibid.
3. Ibid.
4. "Fayette Digs Out From Coal Boom Cave-in," *Pittsburgh Post-Gazette*, 24 November 1990.
5. Ibid.
6. Ibid.
7. Richard Robbins, "Hardy Eager to Get Started," *Tribune-Review* (Pittsburgh), 9 November 2003.
8. Paul Sunyak, "Hardy Serious About Running for Commissioner," *Herald-Standard* (Uniontown, Pennsylvania), 2 March 2003.

9. Ibid.
10. Ibid.
11. Sunyak, "Hardy Serious."
12. Joe Hardy III, interview, 1 October 2003.
13. Conover, interview.
14. Ibid.
15. Amy Karpinsky, "Hardy Takes Control of GOP Contest," *Herald-Standard* (Uniontown, Pennsylvania), 20 May 2003.
16. Ibid.
17. Robbins, "Hardy Eager."
18. Paul Sunyak, " Fayette Commissioner Candidates Detail Platforms," *Herald-Standard* (Uniontown, Pennsylvania), 27 October 2003.
19. Ibid.
20. Robbins, "Hardy Eager."
21. Maley, interview.
22. Paul Sunyak, "Vicites, Hardy, Zimmerlink Win," *Herald-Standard* (Uniontown, Pennsylvania), 5 November 2003.
23. Ibid.
24. Ibid.
25. Ibid.
26. Mike Bucsko, "Hardy Wins in Fayette; Democrats Sweep Allegheny County Row Offices," *Pittsburgh Post-Gazette*, 5 November 2003.
27. Ibid.
28. Joe Hardy III, interview, 12 July 2004.
29. Susan Morgans, "Joe Billionaire," *Mount Lebanon*, April 2004, 29.
30. "Historic Uniontown," Inn at Watson's Choice Web site, www.watsonschoice.com
31. Charmaine Sampson, interview by Jeffrey L. Rodengen, audio recording, 5 November 2004, Write Stuff Enterprises.
32. Steve Neubauer, interview by Jeffrey L. Rodengen, audio recording, 17 November 2004, Write Stuff Enterprises.
33. Sampson, interview.

34. Bob Junk, interview by Jeffrey L. Rodengen, audio recording, 17 November 2004, Write Stuff Enterprises.
35. Neubauer, interview.
36. Junk, interview.
37. Neubauer, interview.
38. Norma Ryan, interview by Jeffrey L. Rodengen, audio recording, 17 November 2004, Write Stuff Enterprises.
39. Joe Ferens, interview by Jeffrey L. Rodengen, audio recording, 30 November 2004, Write Stuff Enterprises.
40. Bill Lincoln, interview by Jeffrey L. Rodengen, audio recording, 9 December 2004, Write Stuff Enterprises.
41. Vince Vicites, interview by Jeffrey L. Rodengen, audio recording, 15 November 2004, Write Stuff Enterprises.
42. "84 Lumber Presents the Boy Scouts of America With a Check for $72,780.00," 84 Lumber news release, 1 August 2003.
43. Ibid.
44. "84 Lumber Company Awards Over $100 Thousand in Scholarships," 84 Lumber news release, 10 March 2003.
45. Ibid.
46. Ibid.
47. Crompton, "Joe Hardy Rebuilding His Empire."
48. "84 Lumber, Biography: Joseph A. Hardy, Sr."
49. Ibid.
50. Washington and Jefferson College Web site, www. washjeff.edu
51. Ibid.
52. Ibid.
53. Ibid.
54. "84 Lumber Teams Up with Local Community to Support Rescued P.O.W., Jessica

Lynch," 84 Lumber news release, 23 April 2003.

55. Ibid.

56. Jim McKinnon and Rhonda Miller, "Playground to Rise Again with Lumber Firm's Help," *Pittsburgh Post-Gazette*, 11 November 2000.

57. Ibid.

58. Ibid.

59. Ibid.

60. Zajac, "For Resort President."

61. Ibid.

62. Joe Hardy III, interview, 12 July 2004.

63. Maley, interview.

64. Joe Hardy III, interview, 12 July 2004.

65. Crompton, "Joe Hardy Rebuilding His Empire."

66. "About 84," 84 Lumber Company Web site, www.84lumber.com

67. Robert Mendelson, "Building a Business," *Pitt*, Spring 2004, 26.

68. Ibid.

69. Frank Cicero, telephone interview by Amy Bush, 6 May 2005, Write Stuff Enterprises.

70. Hardy Magerko, interview.

71. Frank Cicero, interview, 6 May 2005.

72. Fulton, interview.

73. MacKinney, interview.

74. Jack Klema, interview by Jeffrey L. Rodengen, audio recording, 17 February 2004, Write Stuff Enterprises.

75. Dean Martik, interview by Jeffrey L. Rodengen, audio recording, 17 February 2004, Write Stuff Enterprises.

76. Tomshay, interview.

77. Wallach, interview.

78. Sid McAllister, interview by Jeffrey L. Rodengen, audio recording, 12 July 2004, Write Stuff Enterprises.

79. MacKinney, interview.

80. Debbie Hardy, interview.

81. Gravely, interview.

82. Tomshay, interview.

83. Maley, interview.

84. Joseph Alexander Hardy V, interview.

85. Clark, interview.

86. Joe Hardy III, interview, 1 October 2003.

Chapter Ten Sidebar:
A Natural Partnership

1. "A Brief Introduction to Habitat for Humanity International," Habitat for Humanity Web site, www.habitat.org/how/tour/1.html

2. Ibid.

3. "Building of a Third Habitat for Humanity Home; Bills, Choice One and 84 Lumber Join Forces," Buffalo Bills Web site, www.buffalobills.com, 24 September 2002.

4. Monica Haynes, "Our House: Home Quick Home," *Pittsburgh Post-Gazette*, 15 September 1994.

5. "A Brief Introduction."

6. Donohue, interview.

7. Ibid.

8. Monica Haynes, "Habitat Group Building Home in 84 Hours," *Pittsburgh Post-Gazette*, 8 September 1994.

9. Haynes, "Our House."

10. Ibid.

11. Ibid.

12. Ibid.

13. "84 Lumber Sponsors 84-Hour House," *84 Family News*, October 1994.

14. Elizabeth Rudibaugh, correspondence with Anjali Sachdeva, Write Stuff Enterprises.

15. "Habitat for Humanity Receives Support from 84 Lumber," 84 Lumber news release, 22 January 2004.

16. "84 Lumber Donates to Habitat for Humanity of Greater Indianapolis," 84 Lumber news release, 3 March 2004.

INDEX

Page numbers in italics indicate photographs.